around NEW YORK CITY with KIDS

by Mindy Bailin

3rd EDITION
FODOR'S TRAVEL PUBLICATIONS
New York * Toronto * London * Sydney * Auckland

www.fodors.com

Credits
Writer: Mindy Bailin

Editor: Andrea Lehman
Editorial Production: David Downing
Production/Manufacturing: Angela L. McLean

Design: Fabrizio La Rocca, *creative director;*
Tigist Getachew, *senior art director*
Cover Art and Design: Jessie Hartland
Flip Art and Illustration: Rico Lins, Keren Ora Adomoni/
Rico Lins Studio

About the Writer
New Yorker Mindy Bailin is a teacher and mother of three who writes about family, education, and health for many newspapers and magazines across the country. She is the Director of Bet Torah Nursery School in Mt. Kisco, New York.

Fodor's Around New York City with Kids

Copyright © 2005 by Fodors LLC

Third Edition
ISBN 1-4000-1494-8
ISSN 1526–1468

An Important Tip and an Invitation
Although all prices, opening times, and other details in this book are based on information supplied to us at press time, changes occur all the time in the travel world, and Fodor's cannot accept responsibility for facts that become outdated or for inadvertent errors or omissions. So always confirm information when it matters, especially if you're making a detour to visit a specific place. Your experiences—positive and negative—matter to us. If we have missed or misstated something, please write to us. We follow up on all suggestions. Contact the Around New York City with Kids editor at editors@fodors.com or c/o Fodor's at 1745 Broadway, New York, New York 10019.

Special Sales
This book is available for special discounts for bulk purchases for sales promotions or premiums. Special editions, including personalized covers, excerpts of existing books, and corporate imprints, can be created in large quantities for special needs. For more information, write to Special Markets/Premium Sales, 1745 Broadway, MD 6-2, New York, New York 10019, or e-mail specialmarkets@randomhouse.com.

PRINTED IN THE UNITED STATES OF AMERICA
10 9 8 7 6 5 4 3

COUNTDOWN TO GOOD TIMES

GET READY, GET SET!

Go ahead. Take a bite of the Big Apple and count down to fun while you visit the 68 places that appear in this handy-dandy collection of favorite places and spaces to explore. Whether you're day tripping in the city, planning a weekend family getaway, or spending a weeklong vacation here, there's no better place to be than N-Y-C (or the entire metropolitan area surrounding the city, if you really want to know). These 68 great things to do together include sites in Manhattan, as well as Brooklyn, the Bronx, Queens, and Staten Island. A few sights in New Jersey and Westchester and on Long Island are also included. They're only a stone's throw from the Big Apple and worth the trip.

LOOK INSIDE
Each two-page spread in this book describes a great place to take your family. The "tool bar" at the top of the page lists all the particulars: address, phone numbers, admission prices, hours, and age recommendations. "Keep in Mind" boxes give parents special information to help them make the most of their excursion, while "Hey, Kids!" points out cool facts just for kids. "Eats for Kids" helps you find family-friendly restaurants nearby.

Also in the tool bar are Web addresses for most attractions. Some sites offer virtual tours of these great destinations, which may get your family in the mood for a "field trip." Many Web sites also include learning activities, background information on exhibits, and calendars of events, classes, and programs open to the public. It's worth a look before you plan your visit, and after you go, these sites can be great resources for kids who want to learn more.

To get started, just flip through the book, keeping an eye peeled for the Statue of Liberty's magical transformation. It could only happen in New York. You can find places of interest to your family by just leafing through the listings (in alphabetical order) or by looking in the directories in the back of the book. "All Around Town" groups sights by neighborhood, helpful if you're planning to visit more than one attraction or are looking for additional kid-friendly dining choices. (Call ahead for travel directions and parking availability.) "Something for Everyone" groups attractions by type, such as parks and gardens or free attractions.

BE PREPARED

The prices listed in the book are regular adult, student (with ID), and kids' prices; children under the ages specified are free, but there are often ways to get a bargain. When planning your visit, always check local newspapers and family publications for coupons, special discounts, and combination tickets. Many attractions also offer discounts if you belong to an automobile club or other designated organizations. Some places even offer free admission on certain days or at certain times. When in doubt, check it out.

Call ahead to confirm prices, discounts, and hours of operation. The hours listed in this book are an attraction's basic hours, not necessarily those applicable on holidays. Also inquire about the busiest times for these attractions. When school is in session or during summer camp, lines can be long and crowds may be unbearable. On those days, consider a late afternoon visit, after the groups have headed for the buses.

Don't forget the sunscreen and hats for sunny days and outdoor locations, pocket ponchos or folding umbrellas for rain, and the portable stroller or backpack for walking distances with very young children. Be sure to pack water bottles or juice drinks to quench your thirst and a few snacks to hold the group over before your lunch or munch break. Do be mindful of those attractions that prohibit food or drink in exhibit halls or other spaces, though. Most importantly, remember this book. It easily slips into a diaper bag, beach bag, camera case, picnic tote, or purse. Don't leave home without it!

Pace yourself and your family during these excursions. There's no need to see every exhibit in the museum or every animal in the zoo. Focus on a few fun aspects of each attraction. Don't rush. If you have time for further exploration, go for it! But don't expect to cover the entire attraction in your first visit. Plan to come back, especially if this trip is a successful one for your young tourists.

It goes without saying that you should keep a close eye on your children at all times, especially if they're small. To make sure your outing is safe and successful, consider dressing your children in bright, colorful, or same-color shirts or hats. It's not a bad idea for you to do the same, so your children can spot you in a crowd. Pick a visible landmark and a meeting time to reunite just in case you become separated. When you first arrive at your destination, identify staff and security people so everyone knows whom to ask for help or directions if needed.

MAKE IT LAST

The places included and the information provided were carefully chosen to help your family create "teachable moments" and lasting memories for your children. Finding something of interest for everyone is always a challenge, but most of these places appeal to a wide age range—from toddlers to teens, parents to grandparents. To create a "teachable moment" and make a memory last a lifetime, give your child a disposable camera to capture favorite experiences on film. After your excursion, make a family adventure scrapbook or photo album. Older children may want to create a video complete with kid commentary. Handwritten journals or computer-generated diaries are also creative and fun ways to record your family fun, and these family records tend to become priceless.

Did somebody say gift shop? Yes, most of the attractions in this book have some type of retail gift boutique on the premises. To avoid a severe case of the "gimmies," save this stop for right before you go home. Before entering those portals of pricey paraphernalia, agree on the amount of the purchase and hold firm. While a small and charming souvenir can immortalize the day, there's no need to break the bank.

DON'T FORGET TO WRITE

Is there a special attraction in our countdown that your family especially enjoys? Did we overlook one of your favorite places? We'd love to hear from you. Send your e-mails to me c/o editors@fodors.com. Please include "Around New York City with Kids" in the subject line. Or drop me a line by snail mail c/o Around New York City with Kids, Fodor's Travel Publications, 1745 Broadway, New York, NY 10019.

Wherever you go and whatever you do, have a great day. Remember you're exploring the greatest city in the world and you're traveling with the greatest kids in the world...yours.

MINDY BAILIN

AMERICAN FOLK ART MUSEUM

There's something about folk art that appeals to children. Perhaps it's the seeming simplicity, the depictions of everyday objects and creatures, or the frequent flights of whimsy. But whatever the reason, your children will probably enjoy this collection of artworks from the 18th, 19th, and 20th centuries.

In 2001 the museum opened a handsome new building, quadrupling its exhibition space and allowing for enhanced education and programming facilities. The permanent collection highlights America's folk art heritage through paintings, sculpture, furniture, textiles, and decorative arts. Items include dolls, carousel horses, weather vanes, and whirligigs. *Uncle Sam Riding a Bicycle,* a sculpture that moves in the wind, and the colorful *Flag Quilt,* by Mary Baxter, are just two examples of the patriotic art preserved here. The fantastic scroll-like paintings of self-taught 20th-century artist Henry Darger are also part of the permanent display.

KEEP IN MIND This urban museum is special not only for the rich folk heritage of its collection, but also for its free admission for kids and for all on Friday 5:30–7:30—unusual for New York City. The museum's close proximity to Central Park, Carnegie Hall, shopping, and other attractions means you can make a visit here part of a fun-filled day in the heart of the Big Apple.

 45 W. 53rd St.

 212/265–1040;
www.folkartmuseum.org

 $9 ages 13 and up; art
workshop $10 families
(incl. admission)

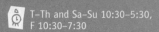 T–Th and Sa–Su 10:30–5:30,
F 10:30–7:30

 2 and up,
art workshop 5 and up

Folk Art Revealed, installed as part of the permanent collection in November 2004, explores the nature of folk art through the themes of symbolism, utility, individuality, and community. New pieces on display include the patriotic *Flag Gate;* the *Freedom Quilt,* created by Jesse Telfair; the whimsical *The Comfort of Moses and the Ten Commandments;* and the towering architectural model *Encyclopedic Palace of the World.*

Temporary exhibits spotlight a particular artist or theme. Guided tours, workshops, puppet shows, concerts, and storytelling take place year-round. Programs are designed in conjunction with exhibitions. Sunday afternoon art workshops, called Folk Art Fun for Families (reservations required), follow guided family tours of the museum. Popular past programs have included self-portraits as animals, sock-and-kitchen-towel people, and 3-D comics. Children join right in.

HEY, KIDS! Ask for a self-guided scavenger hunt at the front desk, and search for the many colorful animals in the collection. *Critters A to Z* is a fun read on sale in the gift shop, aimed at kids 3 and up; it also includes the many animals in the museum.

EATS FOR KIDS The mezzanine level of the main museum features a small **coffee bar.** Close to Lincoln Center, the **Saloon** (1920 Broadway, tel. 212/ 874–1500) has an extensive menu and an occasional skating waiter, or, for a frightfully fun meal, eat at **Jekyll & Hyde** (1409 6th Ave., tel. 212/541–9505).

AMERICAN MUSEUM OF NATURAL HISTORY

This museum, a wonderful place of exploration, discovery, and learning for generations of children, contains more than 30 million specimens and cultural artifacts. Exhibits range from dinosaurs to gems and minerals, from life in the sea to cultures from around the world to the ends of the cosmos.

A good place to begin with young visitors is the six spectacular halls containing the world's most comprehensive and scientifically important dinosaur collection. The five-story exhibit in the Theodore Roosevelt Rotunda, featuring a *Barosaurus* rising up to protect its baby from an *Allosaurus,* is the tallest freestanding dinosaur exhibit on earth. Also making children's eyes sparkle, the Hall of Gems houses the Star of India, the world's largest and most famous blue star sapphire. The Hall of Biodiversity, which opened in 1998, features a multiscreen video projection that gives a global tour of nine ecosystems as well as a 2,500-square-foot diorama that creates a section of an African rain forest. And don't miss the replica of a 95-foot blue whale suspended in the Milstein Hall of Ocean Life. Not that you *could* miss it.

KEEP IN MIND The museum is huge, with 45 exhibition halls in 25 interconnected buildings. It's impossible to see the entire collection in one visit, so keep your focus narrow and plan to return. Each year 4 million people visit, so no matter when you come, you won't be alone.

HEY, KIDS! When was the last time you hunted for hidden creatures in an African baobab tree? Ever piece together the skeleton of a prehistoric *Prestosuchus* (a 14-foot reptile from the late Triassic period) or find fossils in a simulated dinosaur dig? If you haven't and you're up for exploring a hands-on "museum within the museum," then head to the renovated Discovery Room. Here you can get up close and personal with some of the museum's wonders. Older kids can analyze images from the Hubble Telescope and use a seismograph to track earthquakes worldwide, on the mezzanine level. Extremely cool!

Central Park West at 79th St.

212/769-5100, 212/769-5200 museum programs and tickets, 212/769-5993 natural science center; www.amnh.org

  Suggested donation $12 ages 13 and up, $7 children 2–12; museum and space show $19 ages 13 and up, $11 children; IMAX extra

 Daily 10–5:45, space shows Sa–Th 10:30–4:30, F 10:30–7

 2 and up

The Center for Earth and Space, a monumental 120-foot-high, 333,500-square-foot exhibition, research, and education facility, houses the renovated Hayden Planetarium. A gleaming cube of glass envelops the magnificent Hayden Sphere, some 87 feet in diameter. Here the Space Theater screens "The Search for Life," narrated by Harrison Ford, and "Passport to the Universe," narrated by Tom Hanks. On Friday and Saturday evenings, "SonicVision," a digitally animated alternative-music show with a mix by Moby, will captivate your teens. Though museum admission includes the Center for Earth and Space, Hayden Planetarium space shows cost extra and advance tickets are advised.

If you tire of looking at exhibits, check the IMAX movie schedule for larger-than-life films that reveal nature's wonders, shown daily on a four-story screen. But no matter what your game plan, call the museum in advance for information on lectures, performances, workshops, and special family events. There's just so much going on; you won't want to miss a thing.

EATS FOR KIDS The **Museum Food Court** offers a wide variety of food for all ages and palates: stone-oven pizza alongside sushi, pasta, a salad and antipasto bar, grilled sandwiches, and smoothies. The **Cafe on 4** overlooks the grounds at 77th Street from a windowed turret. Selections include sandwiches, salads, fruits, ice-cream desserts, espresso, and cold beverages. **Cafe 77,** in the 77th Street lobby next to the giant Haida canoe, also offers snacks and light bites. For a burger or banana split, take a walk to **EJ's Luncheonette** (447 Amsterdam Ave., tel. 212/873-3444).

AMERICAN MUSEUM OF THE MOVING IMAGE

Lights! Camera! Action! For any fan of film or television, this museum is *the* place to see the nation's most comprehensive public collection of film and video artifacts. From Thomas Edison's Projecting Kinescope (circa 1897) to computer files used to design film sets in the 1990s, from the earliest existing television receiver (1927) to the most recent computer games, the museum has a wealth of materials from motion pictures, TV, and digital media.

The core exhibition, Behind the Screen, explores how motion pictures and TV programs are created, how they find their audiences, and how their place in our culture has evolved. Displays include such tools of the trade as cameras, microphones, and video recorders, and 13 interactive stations let you try to create a short animated movie, apply sound effects to famous movie scenes, and perform in front of a blue screen just like a TV weatherperson.

Among the collection of moving-image artifacts are costumes, posters, cameras, projectors, stage sets, fan magazines, and licensed merchandise. You can view the original Yoda puppet

KEEP IN MIND The museum offers a number of programs to enhance your visit. Movie-making exhibits are especially engaging when explained by a tour guide. Free tours are given weekends at 2, along with live demonstrations of filmmaking techniques, such as editing and animation; call ahead to reserve space. Also ask about special events, such as guest speakers. Each year an array of famous film and TV actors, directors, and filmmakers make personal appearances at the museum to discuss their craft. Though these are primarily of interest to adults, some will certainly interest kids, especially teenagers. Guest speakers have included the late cartoonist Chuck Jones and director Spike Lee.

 35th Ave. and 36th St.,
Astoria, Queens

 $10 adults, $5 children 5–18

W–Th 12–5, F 12–8, Sa–Su 11–6:30

718/784–0077;
www.ammi.org

5 and up

from *The Empire Strikes Back*, a mechanical Linda Blair from *The Exorcist*, vintage TV sets, and dolls of famous movie and TV characters, including Mr. T, Batman, Urkel, and the Simpsons. Where else can you see a gold-plated chariot from the 1959 film *Ben-Hur* alongside a collection of Fonzie paper dolls?

The museum occupies a 60,000-square-foot building across from the 13-acre Kaufman Astoria Studios complex, where *Sesame Street* is produced. Look for the address the next time Big Bird rolls the credits. Each year in the intimate 200-seat Riklis Theater, more than 400 screenings of TV programs and videotapes are presented in their original formats. Silent films are shown with live musical accompaniment. And don't pass up the neo-Egyptian Tut's Fever Movie Palace, a spoof on a 1920s theater, where hourly movie serials and shorts are screened. Since the films and videos are free, for about the cost of a movie in New York, you can have quite an experience here.

HEY, KIDS! In addition to letting you make an animated short, those interactive stations enable you to dub dialogue, create a flipbook starring yourself, or project your image onto the costumes of famous stars. You can even see how your dad would look as John Travolta in *Saturday Night Fever*.

EATS FOR KIDS You can catch a light bite in the **museum's café.** For lunch, dinner, snacks, or dessert, Broadway between 31st and 35th streets offers a large selection of restaurants and cafés within walking distance. A good choice for diner delights and Greek food, **Uncle George's** (33–19 Broadway, tel. 718/626–0593) is open 24 hours. Or follow the aroma of coffee and pastry to an outdoor table at a local pastry shop for baklava or other sweet treats.

ASPHALT GREEN

It has Manhattan's only Olympic-standard pool that's open to the public, not to mention a separate teaching and exercise pool, a regulation AstroTurf field for sports, two gyms, an indoor and outdoor running track, two outdoor parks, the Mazur Hall theater, and indoor and outdoor basketball courts. Whew! Are we finished yet? Not quite. Add to that a duplex fitness center, aerobics rooms, a physical-therapy/health center, and graphics, photography, and fine artist studios. Get the feeling it's worth visiting this campuslike, 5½-acre sports and training complex? Absolutely. And what does "asphalt" have to do with "green," anyway?

Established in 1968 where a former municipal asphalt plant once operated, Asphalt Green was created as a recreational center for city youth and the community at large. The parabolic plant building was declared a New York City landmark and today serves as a full-service sports and fitness complex. The city still owns the land, but in return for rental exemption, Asphalt Green provides a third of its services free to the community.

KEEP IN MIND Birthday party options include puppet shows, gymnastics, swimming, and other sports themes. A decorated room, paper goods, helium balloons, and a party host are provided. You supply the refreshments, guests, and, of course, the birthday child. No fuss, no mess, no bother.

HEY, KIDS! Each fall the Asphalt Games mean sports and fun, with clinics hosted by Olympians. Kids under 3 can visit Toddler Village. Proceeds support community partnership programs. In spring, meet Olympic swimmers, earn a medal, and get cool free stuff at the annual Big Swim. Top swimmers in each event are invited to participate in an AquaShow, featuring some of the country's best swimmers, lights, music, and a cast of kids. But no matter how good a swimmer you are, if you're ages 6 to 16 you can make a big splash and help raise money for Asphalt Green's Waterproofing program, which teaches thousands of city kids to swim for free.

 555 E. 90th St.

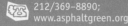 212/369–8890;
www.asphaltgreen.org

 Swim session $25 ages 17 and up, $8 children 16 and under; puppet playhouse $6 ages 11 mos. and up

 M–F 5:30 AM–10 PM, Sa–Su 8–8; puppet playhouse Sa 10:30, 12, 1:30

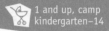 1 and up, camp kindergarten–14

As for the "green" portion of its name, the complex also contains Dekovats and Sundial Plaza parks, which feature plenty of green space and gardens, park benches, and game tables. Dekovats adds a playground and a sprinkler in summer, whereas Sundial Plaza has a fountain.

Children's classes are held in aquatics, sports and fitness, music, and art. Offerings are varied and include swimming, diving, synchronized swimming, soccer, gymnastics, karate, and yoga. Private lessons are also available. Summer camp activities include sports and various arts: of the "fine," "performing," "crafts," and "martial" varieties. Holiday mini-camps and sports clinics are held throughout the year and during school breaks.

The Lenny Suib Puppet Playhouse at Asphalt Green's Mazur Hall stages performances with hand puppets, rod puppets, shadow puppets, marionettes, ventriloquists, magicians, storytellers, and clowns as well as exciting guest artists. About the only thing you can't do here anymore is make asphalt.

EATS FOR KIDS For healthy sandwiches, salads, and smoothies, not to mention kid-friendly snacks, visit Asphalt Green's **Wave Café.** The gourmet soups are winners, too. A popular food emporium is the **Vinegar Factory** (431 E. 91st St., tel. 212/628–9608). Come for brunch, breakfast, lunch, or dinner for fabulous sandwiches, soups, salads, and pastas. For seafood, barbecued chicken, ribs, and pork, not to mention a kids-eat-free deal every night of the week, you can't beat **Brother Jimmy's Bait Shack** (1644 3rd Ave., tel. 212/426–2020).

BROADWAY ON A BUDGET

With tickets for top shows costing up to $100 each, it can be expensive to give your family's regards to Broadway. Enter TKTS. At two locations—Duffy Square (Times Square) and South Street Seaport—you can purchase discounted tickets to Broadway and Off-Broadway plays and musicals. (Off-Broadway is usually cheaper.) The names of available shows are posted by the booths. You probably won't get tickets to the season's smash hit—after all, they're only made available to TKTS if the theater isn't sold out—but there will undoubtedly be something that's entertaining and/or enlightening.

Lines are usually shorter at the South Street Seaport location, and matinee tickets are sold a day in advance. The wait on the often long line at Duffy Square usually moves fast, however, and if you get your tickets here, you'll be halfway there. You can kill time around Times Square, grab a bite, and walk to the theater. Remember to bring cash or traveler's checks, because TKTS doesn't take American Express—or other credit cards.

KEEP IN MIND Most theaters are dark one day of the week, usually Monday, so plan your theater excursion accordingly. Scoring tickets for Tuesday through Thursday evening performances and Wednesday matinees is often easiest. Also check for those shows now offering an early (7 PM) curtain time on Tuesday. If you're wondering what a show is about, where it's playing, who's in it, whether it's okay for kids, and how long it lasts, call the Broadway Line (*see above*), run by the League of American Theatres and Producers, or visit www.LiveBroadway.com for information on current performances.

TKTS, Duffy Sq., 47th St. and Broadway; South Street Seaport, 199 Water St.

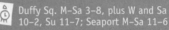 Duffy Sq. M–Sa 3–8, plus W and Sa 10–2, Su 11–7; Seaport M–Sa 11–6

 Usually 50%–75% off regular price plus $2.50 surcharge per ticket

 212/768–1818, 888/BROADWAY Broadway Line; www.livebroadway.com, www.kidsnightonbroadway.com

 4 and up, but varies by show

For the best tickets, get on line early; many people arrive an hour before the booth opens. To avoid a wait, however, go later in the day, but know that many of the day's offerings may be gone. In fall and nonholiday winter weeks, as many as 50 shows can be available, so don't despair. Family fare can usually be found. Though ticket sellers won't stop and chat about seat locations, the computer automatically lists the "best available" seats. It's likely that your family can sit together, though at the most popular shows, it may be necessary to split into twos and threes.

Another inexpensive way to see well-known long-running shows is to look for bookmark-shape discount coupons, called "twofers." They're distributed by store cash registers, near the TKTS lines, and sometimes in elementary and preschool offices. Twofers enable you to buy two tickets for the price of one for selected days and times. Some theaters also sell discounted seats for unsold tickets a half hour before the curtain goes up.

HEY, KIDS! Each winter theaters open their doors for kids to see a Broadway show for free. Just bring a full-paying adult to specially designated performances. For more information on this cool annual event, called Kids Night on Broadway, visit the Web site, www.kidsnightonbroadway.com.

EATS FOR KIDS For sports fans and those with a craving for a good ballpark frank, score a great lunch at the **ESPN Zone** (1472 Broadway, at 42nd St., tel. 212/921–3776). For home-style Italian pastas and chicken and veal dishes like mama used to make, served family style, you can't go wrong at **Carmine's** (200 W. 44th St., between Broadway and 8th Ave., tel. 212/221–3800). Choose from 17 burger toppings or split a gargantuan sandwich at the **Stage Deli** (834 7th Ave., tel. 212/245–7850). Don't forget the pickles. Also see NBC Studios Tour, the New Victory Theater, Radio City Music Hall, and Rockefeller Center and the Ice Rink.

BRONX ZOO

The Bronx Zoo is the country's largest metropolitan wildlife park, home to more than 4,500 animals, including endangered and threatened species. But the exhibits here aren't fenced areas containing standard zoo animals. One example is the World of Darkness, where your children are suddenly up way past their bedtimes to get a "night view" of such nocturnal animals as leopard cats, cloud rats, and bats. Kids can peek at a subterranean naked mole rat colony or watch big and beautiful endangered cats through the glass at Tiger Mountain, the newest not-to-be-missed exhibit. Keepers do daily demonstrations with the Siberian tigers as well as Tiger Talks three times daily.

The 265-acre zoo is too big to cover in a day and big enough to warrant returning again and again. With young children, begin in the north in parking lot B (the only year-round lot). Walk west to the Monkey House (or come at 3:30 for a small-primate training session), loop around the elephants, and land at the Children's Zoo, where learning about animals occurs by doing what animals do. Youngsters can climb a giant spider's web,

HEY, KIDS!

For a bird's-eye view of the park, ride the Skyfari aerial cable car or the awesome Bengali Express monorail (May–October). Head to these first because lines can get long. Look for the World of Reptiles, the only building that was here on the zoo's opening day, November 8, 1899, and has its original use.

KEEP IN MIND
Summer sees the biggest crowds, and many exhibits—the monorail, Skyfari, camel rides, and Zoo Shuttle—are open only in warm months. (With toddlers, sit in the monorail's back row, so wee ones are high enough to see.) The Children's Zoo is also open during Holiday Lights, mid-November–December. Not surprisingly, human animals, like the animals they've come to see, don't always enjoy the heat. In hot (or cold) weather, visit the indoor, temperature-controlled exhibits. Feeding times make animals more active. Sea lions eat at 11 and 3 except on Wednesday, penguins at 3:30. Strollers are a must, and rentals—including those for adults—are available.

Bronx River Pkwy.
and Fordham Rd., Bronx

718/367-1010;
www.wcs.org

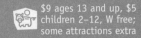
$9 ages 13 and up, $5
children 2–12, W free;
some attractions extra

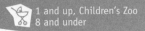
Apr–Oct, M–F 10–5, Sa–Su 10–5:30; Nov–Mar,
daily 10–4:30; Children's Zoo Apr–Oct

1 and up, Children's Zoo
8 and under

try on a turtle shell, or escape like a lizard down a hollow tree, exploring five themed areas, including the one where they can pet and feed domesticated animals. If attention spans hold, walk north to the Aquatic Bird House (2:45 brings a cricket toss to the bee eaters at the World of Birds) and east past the bison before leaving.

For older children, begin in Asia Parking A (April–October), to the zoo's south. Walk to Wild Asia to experience JungleWorld, a major indoor exhibit that re-creates an Indonesian scrub forest, mangrove forest, and Southeast Asian rain forest with about 780 animals representing 99 species. Next walk northwest past the nyalas to Africa to visit the Carter Giraffe Building before heading north to the Baboon Reserve, which re-creates the Ethiopian highland habitat of the gelada baboon. Walk west past the ostriches and storks to the Congo Gorilla Forest, a 6.5-acre indoor/outdoor African rain forest, which takes visitors into the world of endangered lowland gorillas, colorful mandrills, African rock pythons, rare okapis, red river hogs, colobus monkeys, and other spectacular species. It's a must-see.

EATS FOR KIDS Snack stands are located throughout the park, selling (often overpriced) drinks, ice cream, and every other zoo snack imaginable. For more substantial fare, eat at the **Asia Plaza, Terrace Café,** or **African Market** (overlooking the Baboon Reserve); these locations are open seasonally. The **Dancing Crane Café,** open year-round, features a contemporary menu that includes fresh pizza, salads, sandwiches, wraps, and Italian entrées. The café can seat 210 indoors and 824 outdoors, overlooking the flamingo pond. Tables are available for those who pack a picnic.

BROOKLYN ACADEMY OF MUSIC

Founded in 1861, the Brooklyn Academy of Music (BAM) is America's oldest performing arts center, presenting a full schedule of traditional and contemporary performing arts in the fields of dance, music, theater, opera, and cinema.

Public programs include BAMfamily weekend performances and spoken-word performances by and for teens. This great introduction to dance, music, and theater in beautiful theaters at affordable prices appeals to tots, teens, and parents alike. Performances are chosen to meet several criteria, including cultural diversity, multidisciplinary appeal, exposure to theatrical innovation, and the extent to which the performance is likely to introduce a young audience to art forms they may not have had the opportunity to experience before.

The Brooklyn Academy of Music also presents an annual BAMkids Film Festival, in the main building's BAM Rose Cinemas. Offerings range from animated shorts of four to seven minutes to feature films running 1½ to 2 hours.

HEY, KIDS! Part of the fun of the spring BAMkids Film Festival is watching movies from other lands. A recent festival included 46 live-action and animated films from 22 countries including France, Brazil, Peru, the Netherlands, India, Taiwan, and Cameroon. But don't worry if you can't speak the language. Many foreign films have English subtitles, and for most of these films, actors read the subtitles out loud. The festival also includes live performances, discussions with filmmakers, and the BAMmies, where kids vote for their favorite films.

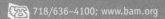
Every Memorial Day, DanceAfrica presents dance ensembles from around the world. More than 200 vendors transform the streets surrounding BAM into a global bazaar of African, Caribbean, and African-American crafts, food, clothing, and toys. Summertime means free R&B concerts at Brooklyn's downtown MetroTech Center and in area parks. Be sure to mark your calendar for the Halloween trick or treat event with candy, entertainment, and costume competitions!

Created in 1908, BAM's main building is the home of the 2,000-seat Howard Gilman Opera House and the 750-seat quad cineplex BAM Rose Cinemas. In addition to food, the BAMcafé serves up live jazz on Friday and Saturday nights. The BAM Harvey Theater is a renovated historic space two blocks from the main facility, at 651 Fulton Street. But whichever event you attend, the academy's performances will take your family on a memorable artistic journey. Bam!

EATS FOR KIDS
When there are family events at BAM, the **BAMcafé** (tel. 718/636-4139) opens at 4 for dinner, earlier for concessions on matinee days. **Cino's** (243 DeKalb Ave., tel. 718/622-9249) is the place for tried-and-true home-cooked Italian food. Side portions of pasta are kid-pleasers.

GETTING THERE To reach BAM by car, take the Manhattan Bridge to Flatbush Avenue, and turn left onto Fulton Street. For the Harvey Theater, parking is on your right; for the Opera House, proceed two blocks on Fulton, and turn right onto Ashland Place. Parking is one block ahead on the right. (Hint: it's cheaper for subscribers and Friends of BAM.) If you're coming by subway, take the 2, 3, 4, 5, B, or Q line to Atlantic Avenue; the D, N, R, or M line to Pacific Street; the G line to Fulton Street; or C line to Lafayette Avenue.

BROOKLYN BOTANIC GARDEN

It's easy to spend a day in this 52-acre blooming paradise with more than 10,000 plants outside and under glass. In fact, it's easy to spend several days a year. There's something different to see each season: the Zen-like tranquillity of the Japanese Hill and Pond Garden in fall, the puffy white winter pussy willows and early bulbs bursting with color in the Rock Garden in February, a spring flowering festival of tulips, and sunny summer garden delights.

The Discovery Garden is an outdoor adventure for kids, especially preschoolers, but filled with fun for everyone. It's immediately inside the Flatbush Avenue entrance at the south end of the garden. Your children can look through "bug-eye" lenses or blaze a trail through a bamboo forest, butterfly garden, meadow, maze, grassy areas, and a nature trail. Brightly colored Plant Discovery carts are stocked with games, puzzles, art supplies, and natural objects. (Topics and activities change regularly.) Carts also dispense free Family Fun kits for more exploration at home. Other favorite places in the botanical garden include the Fragrance Garden, where low beds are easily accessible for visitors in wheelchairs and

HEY, KIDS!
The Children's Garden here was the first one in a botanical garden and the oldest continuously operating one in the world; 800 kids garden here every year, including KinderGardeners (ages 3–6). The Planting Day Parade and Harvest Celebration are favorite events in this program of planting, tending, craft-making, and play.

KEEP IN MIND Special family events occur year-round. The fall Chili Pepper Fiesta often includes puppet shows, strolling mariachis, interactive storytelling, paper crafts, and face painting. The Cherry Blossom Festival fairly blooms with activities for children in spring, often including musical performances, martial-arts demonstrations, haiku readings, Japanese storytelling, Japanese printing workshops, doll-making, origami, and calligraphy.

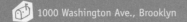 1000 Washington Ave., Brooklyn

 718/623-7200, 718/623-7220
Discovery Programs; www.bbg.org

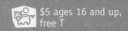 $5 ages 16 and up,
free T

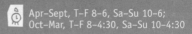 Apr–Sept, T–F 8–6, Sa–Su 10–6;
Oct–Mar, T–F 8–4:30, Sa–Su 10–4:30

 All ages

little ones. It's the only place aside from the Discovery Garden where you're encouraged to touch the plants. Afterward, you can rinse the smells off your fingers in a small fountain.

The Celebrity Path is paved with stones inscribed with the names of famous Brooklynites past and present. How many can you recognize? The Japanese Hill and Pond Garden is home to ducks, turtles, koi, and herons, which can be surveyed from the Viewing Pavilion. Shrines, bridges, and waterfalls complete a miniaturized landscape that appeals to children. A restoration of this area has resulted in better paths for strollers and wheelchairs. It's a great place for kids to see wildlife.

For a more hands-on approach, consider the drop-in Discovery Programs: Sunday workshops for 3- to 10-year-olds and 15-minute workshops on Tuesday for 3- to 6-year-olds. Sessions are held in the Discovery Garden or the Chase Manhattan Discovery Center, and topics change monthly.

EATS FOR KIDS Picnicking isn't allowed in the garden. In fact Cherry Esplanade is the only place where sitting on the grass is even permitted. So to eat on the grounds, you have to go to the **Terrace Café,** which offers lunch outdoors from spring to early fall and in the Steinhardt Conservatory late fall and winter. For deli sandwiches and cheesecake, take a short ride to **Junior's Restaurant** (386 Flatbush Ave., tel. 718/852–5257), a classic '50s diner. Also see the Brooklyn Museum of Art, Prospect Park, and the Prospect Park Zoo. Outside the garden's south entrance are two fast-food hamburger restaurants.

BROOKLYN CHILDREN'S MUSEUM

Enter through a corrugated metal tunnel lit with neon bands and you immediately know you're on your way to an innovative, educational, fun, and fabulous place for kids. Of course, that's not how you would have entered the world's first museum for children when it was founded in 1899. Over the years, this century-old museum has served as a model for other children's museums worldwide, thanks to interactive exhibits, kids' programs, workshops, and performances.

Upon arrival, check the daily information board to see what workshops and programs are planned. Then head to any of the 10 galleries, which incorporate musical traditions, nature experiments, live animals, collections, and computers to create exhibits that tickle the imaginations of young and old. On any given day, your children may be able to assemble an 8-foot-high elephant skeleton puzzle, play musical instruments from around the world, pet a snake from the live animal collection, or experiment with plants in the greenhouse. Highlights of the museum's 27,000-object permanent collection range from masks, sculpture,

KEEP IN MIND The third weekend of every month brings the MetLife Early Learner Performance Series, for children 5 and younger, and Early Learner Workshops in science, creative play, and art, from 11 to 12:30. The Planet Brooklyn culture series spotlights a different culture every month with the celebration of a special holiday, festival, or tradition. Free Friday Rooftop Jam offers dance and theater performances every Friday evening in summer.

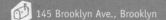 145 Brooklyn Ave., Brooklyn

 Suggested donation $4

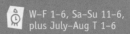 W–F 1–6, Sa–Su 11–6, plus July–Aug T 1–6

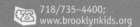 718/735-4400; www.brooklynkids.org

 2 and up

instruments, and adornments from African, Central American, Asian, and Oceanic cultures to such natural history specimens as dinosaur footprints, mammoth teeth, an elephant skeleton, and a whale rib. A famous collection of dolls runs the gamut from folk dolls to a 36-piece set of Queen Elizabeth II coronation dolls designed by Madame Alexander.

Your kids can run a pizza shop in the Together in the City exhibit, which re-creates a festive urban community. Visit the popular Animal Outpost, where you can meet Fantasia, the 17-foot-long albino Burmese python. The Totally Tots gallery is dedicated to early learning for toddlers. Three theaters include an outdoor rooftop amphitheater where performances from around the world are regularly featured. You might have noticed a strong global emphasis here; along with focusing on a wealth of cultures, this place offers a world of fun.

EATS FOR KIDS
For plentiful home cooking, try the **New Prospect Cafe** (393 Flatbush Ave., tel. 718/638–2148). The **Lemongrass Grill** (61A 7th Ave., tel. 718/399–7100) is a link in a reasonably priced Thai food chain. Ask the kitchen to go light on the spices. Also see the Brooklyn Museum.

HEY, KIDS! The Brooklyn Children's Museum is about to grow. The new building, set to open in 2007, will double the museum's size and is slated to be the first "green" children's museum in the nation. No, that doesn't mean the building will be green! It means the museum will use environmentally friendly materials and systems. But not to worry–you will still be able to enjoy all the museum has to offer even during the construction period.

BROOKLYN MUSEUM

59

It's the second-largest museum in New York State, established in 1823, and considered one of the premier art institutions in the world. Is it in Manhattan? No, it was born and bred—and still lives—in Brooklyn. It's the Beaux Arts–style Brooklyn Museum. More than 1 million objects range from the art of ancient Egypt to contemporary painting and sculpture, and the museum's collections of Asian, American, Egyptian, Native American, and African art are recognized as some of the best in the world.

There are all kinds of ways to enjoy the museum with children. If you're bound for the African Galleries, pick up a "Family Guide" at the information desk to help explain what you can see. Weekend family programs, which are free, include storytelling by guests from around the world; special dance, opera, and other music performances; and meet-the-author or -illustrator seminars. During the school year, weeklong programs are conducted for grade schoolers.

EATS FOR KIDS The **Museum Café** is open almost as long as the museum, or try the **Second Street Café** (see the Prospect Park Zoo). For a snack and a drink, try **Ozzie's Coffee & Tea** (57 7th Ave., tel. 718/398–6695), an interesting converted drugstore with apothecary cases.

HEY, KIDS! At the Learning Center, explore the Brooklyn Expedition (www.brooklynexpedition.org), a nifty Web site developed by this museum, the Brooklyn Children's Museum, and the Brooklyn Public Library. It's a great resource containing pictures and articles about objects, exhibits, and collections plus interactive activities. Once you're back at home or school—or if you can only make a virtual museum visit—you can access the site for help on projects or just for fun. Your museum experience will never end.

200 Eastern Pkwy.,
Brooklyn

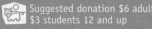
Suggested donation $6 adults,
$3 students 12 and up

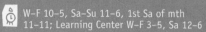
W–F 10–5, Sa–Su 11–6, 1st Sa of mth
11–11; Learning Center W–F 3–5, Sa 12–6

718/638–5000;
www.brooklynart.org

4 and up, Arty Facts 4–7, Gallery/
Studio Program 6 and up

The Gallery/Studio Program offers students the opportunity to study the museum's diverse collections as well as work in the studio on their own art. Courses in drawing, painting, sculpture, abstract art, printmaking, collage, and mixed media are offered in 10-week sessions.

At the Learning Center, in the first-floor Education Gallery, you and your children can browse in the museum's children's books and CD-ROMs. If you're visiting on a weekend, be sure to stop by Arty Facts (both days at 11 and 2), a drop-in program that lets children explore the galleries, take part in a family activity, and create their own art using fun themes— all in 1½ hours. Parents of hearing-impaired children can call ahead for a schedule of sign language–interpreted programs. As your children will discover, there's a lot more to do here than simply wander around looking at paintings, though they'll probably find that pretty special, too.

KEEP IN MIND The museum is near the Brooklyn Botanic Garden (*see #61*), the main branch of the Brooklyn Public Library, and Prospect Park and its zoo (*see #s17 and 16*). Although you could easily spend a day at the museum, it's probably better, especially with young children, to keep your first visit short. Spend half a day here, wander to 7th Avenue for lunch at one of the restaurants or cafés, and visit another nearby destination in the afternoon. It'll break up the day and leave your children with a good memory of the museum.

CARNEGIE HALL

How do you get to Carnegie Hall? Practice...practice...or just attend one of the family concerts held throughout the year on weekend afternoons on this world-famous stage and in the new Zankel Hall, located underneath the main hall. The family concert series, begun in 1995, introduces children to classical, jazz, and folk music at affordable, family-friendly prices. Preconcert activities on the main stage and in other smaller Carnegie Hall spaces include storytelling, hands-on musical experiences, and instrument demonstrations. Concertgoers also receive a special "KidsNotes" program specially designed for youngsters, with activities and information about each family concert.

Another wonderful concert program called CarnegieKIDS is designed to introduce music to preschool children. It's available to nursery schools, day care centers, kindergarten classes, Headstart programs, and small groups but is also open to families; advance registration is required for everyone. These concerts are not held in the main hall, however, but rather in the Kaplan space on the fifth floor.

KEEP IN MIND Can't get to Carnegie Hall? Let Carnegie Hall come to you! Since 1976, the Neighborhood Concert Series has hosted free one-hour community concerts in public libraries, community and senior centers, and shelters in all five New York City boroughs. A variety of artists and ensembles performing repertoires from classical and jazz to folk and pop make up each Neighborhood Concert season. Some of these concerts are Workshop Concerts or Kids Concerts. Seating is on a first-come, first-served basis.

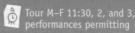

154 W. 57th St., at 7th Ave.

212/247-7800, 212/903-9670
CarnegieKIDS; www.carnegiehall.org

Family concerts $5;
CarnegieKIDS $3; tour
$9 adults, $6 students,
$3 children 11 and under

Tour M–F 11:30, 2, and 3,
performances permitting

Family concerts 5 and up,
CarnegieKIDS 3–6, tour 7 and up

To make a concert experience special for children, it might help to discuss any famous musicians that you or other family members have seen perform here. Headliners have been playing Carnegie Hall since 1891, when its opening concert series included none other than Tchaikovsky conducting his own works. Since then, the hall has attracted the world's finest orchestras and solo and group performers, from Arturo Toscanini and Leonard Bernstein to Duke Ellington, Ella Fitzgerald, Judy Garland, Frank Sinatra, Bob Dylan, and the Beatles.

One-hour guided tours of the hall are also given. And if your kids want to get a close-up look at Benny Goodman's clarinet or catch a glimpse of Arturo Toscanini's baton, visit the Rose Museum, open daily 11–4:30 as well as to concert patrons in the evening. East of the main auditorium, this small museum displays interesting mementos from Carnegie Hall's rich history, and admission is free.

HEY, KIDS! Movie buffs may remember that *Home Alone 2* takes place in New York City and that the lady who feeds the pigeons lives in the attic of—you guessed it—Carnegie Hall. Of course, there's no truth to the rumor that she still lives here. That's only in the movies.

EATS FOR KIDS Before or after a concert or at intermission, visit the **Citigroup Café,** on the Parquet level, for light fare or desserts, or whistle a happy tune over to **Brooklyn Diner USA** (212 W. 57th St., tel. 212/581–8900). Go for the generous portions of kid and comfort foods or the decadent diner desserts. Keep your eyes on the fries, or try stargazing. It's a local celebrity spot. You can order a mile-high sandwich or classic cheesecake at the famous **Carnegie Deli** (854 7th Ave., tel. 212/757–2245).

CASTLE CLINTON NATIONAL MONUMENT

Like any good castle, Castle Clinton has a long history. It was built before the beginning of the War of 1812 to defend the city from sea assault, but no attack ever came. Today you can admire the views of the Statue of Liberty and Ellis Island while your children look for gun turrets and scan the stone walls, imagining themselves soldiers defending a city.

Originally named the Southwest Battery, this circular redbrick fortress served as U.S. Army headquarters during the War of 1812. It had a timber causeway with a drawbridge connecting the fort to Manhattan and was equipped with 28 guns and a magazine inside the rounded ends of the rear wall. In 1817 it was renamed to honor the city's mayor, DeWitt Clinton. Today National Park Service rangers dressed in period costume are available to answer questions, and exhibits tell of the setting's many lives.

It's hard to imagine a more varied history. In 1824 the site was turned into an elegant entertainment facility known as Castle Garden, where the "Swedish Nightingale," Jenny

EATS FOR KIDS For dependable, kid-friendly fare—burgers, wraps, and fajitas—try **T.G.I. Friday's** (47 Broadway, tel. 212/483–8322). Over a mile—but a reasonable cab ride—away, **South Street Seaport** (Water and South Sts.) has an array of fast-food stalls at Pier 17's third-floor food court.

HEY, KIDS! How did the location and design of Castle Clinton help guard the coast of our young country? Notice that Castle Williams, on Governor's Island, is opposite Castle Clinton. Why were these two forts built so near each other? And why do you think Castle Clinton is designed in the shape of a capital D, a circle flattened on the land side? If enemy ships were moving up the East River, how could Castle Clinton help stop this attack?

Battery Park

 Free

 Daily 8:30–5

 212/344-7220;
www.nps.gov/cacl

 4 and up

Lind, sang in 1850. From 1855 to 1890, it served as a receiving station for more than 8 million immigrants and from 1896 to 1941 housed the New York Aquarium. Today it functions as a restored fort, museum, and ticket office for ferries to the Statue of Liberty and Ellis Island. Take a self-guided tour (20–30 minutes) or join ranger-led tours or programs (20–60 minutes). A kiosk on the parade grounds has an information desk and a bookstore filled with books on the history of New York.

Look for the bronze statue titled *The Immigrants,* depicting a Jewish man bent in prayer with his family, along with a priest, a freed African-American slave, a worker, and a child. Paying homage to the immigrants who passed through here, it's at the beginning of a wide expanse that leads to the Netherlands Memorial Flagpole, which commemorates a different era of the site's history—the Dutch purchase of the land for Fort Amsterdam from Native Americans. In all, more than 300 years of history can be discovered here.

KEEP IN MIND Castle Clinton is only one of six historic National Park Service units in New York City. The others include Federal Hall National Memorial and the Theodore Roosevelt Birthplace (*see* #s 45 and 3), St. Paul's National Historic Site, General Grant National Memorial, and the Hamilton Grange National Memorial. In addition to its other functions, Castle Clinton is a visitor center for the city's national parks.

CENTRAL PARK

Central Park is to New York as the sun is to the solar system. This green oasis of over 840 acres is a magnet for families, joggers, bikers, strollers (on foot and wheels), skaters, sunbathers, and people-watchers. Where else in the city can you go horseback riding, boating, ice-skating, roller skating, folk dancing, fishing, and bird-watching; visit the zoo; and attend a play, puppet show, concert, and ball game—though probably not in one day? Weekends are busy here (but crowds make it safe), and free entertainment is everywhere. Go to the Dairy Visitors Center and Gift Shop (65th St., mid-park, tel. 212/794-6564) for park merchandise, maps, and information. Head to 67th Street and 5th Avenue for the tree house playground. A playground at 99th Street (east side) accommodates children with disabilities. Other playgrounds are on the east side at 71st, 77th, 85th, 95th, 108th, and 110th streets and on the west side at 68th, 81st, 85th, 89th, 91st, 93rd, 96th, 100th, and 110th streets.

On land: Ride the 1903 Friedsam Memorial Carousel (Center Dr. and 65th St., tel. 212/879-0244). Belvedere Castle (79th St. Transverse, tel. 212/772-0210), home of a weather station

KEEP IN MIND It's not just couples who like horse-drawn carriage rides. Kids love them, too. You can see the carriages assembled on Central Park South (59th St. between 5th Ave. and Ave. of the Americas) and outside Tavern on the Green. Each is decorated distinctively, and the drivers, too, are a colorful group. Some even sport top hats. Day and evening rides are available for about $34 for 20 minutes for up to four passengers. For more information, contact Central Park Carriage Rides (tel. 212/246-0520). As long as you're home by midnight, the carriage won't turn into a pumpkin and your little Cinderella will stay queen of the ball.

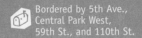
Bordered by 5th Ave.,
Central Park West,
59th St., and 110th St.

212/360-3444;
www.centralparknyc.org

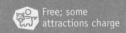
Free; some
attractions charge

Daily sunrise–sunset

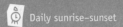
All ages

and the Henry Luce Nature Observatory, houses nature exhibits and programs. Swedish Cottage (79th St. Transverse, tel. 212/988–9093), an 1876 schoolhouse, holds marionette performances. The North Meadow Recreation Center (97th St., mid-park, tel. 212/348–4867) has health, fitness, sports, and adventure programs, plus a climbing wall.

On or near water: At Conservatory Water (off 5th Ave. at 74th St.), children pose by literary statues. Summer storytelling takes place Saturday at 11, model boat races Saturday at 10 spring–fall. At the Charles A. Dana Discovery Center (5th Ave. and 110th St.), borrow poles and bait and head to Harlem Meer for catch-and-release fishing. To skate on frozen water, try the Wollman Memorial Rink (6th Ave. at 59th St., tel. 212/396–1010), mid-October–March (in-line skating April–September), or Lasker Rink (off Lenox Ave. and 110th St., tel. 212/534–7639)—a pool in summer. Tired yet?

HEY, KIDS! The park celebrated its 150th birthday in 2003, but you can find attractions here spanning several millennia. On the old side, Cleopatra's Needle, a hieroglyphic-covered obelisk east of the Great Lawn near the Metropolitan Museum of Art, dates to 1600 BC. Egypt gave it to New York City in 1881.

EATS FOR KIDS Try the **Loeb Boathouse Cafe** (*see* the Central Park Zoo), a seasonal open-air restaurant on the water; a nearby cafeteria serving breakfast and lunch; or the **Sheep Meadow Café** (Central Park West at 69th St., tel. 212/396–4100), also called Mineral Springs. For a splurge, visit famous **Tavern on the Green** (Central Park West at 67th St., tel. 212/873–3200). Twinkling lights, glitzy glass, and mirrors captivate young audiences. Pre-theater specials are reasonable, but reservations are a must.

CENTRAL PARK ZOO

By 1864, captive animals could be found in Central Park. (Of course, wild animals were here earlier, as they are today—with varying numbers of feet.) In 1934, this Animal Menagerie was remodeled, becoming the first Central Park Zoo. It was renovated again in 1980, this time by the Wildlife Conservation Society, an international conservation organization. Approximately 1,500 animals represent more than 120 species in the 6½-acre zoo, a perfect destination for little ones. It's walkable and stroller-friendly, and even the youngest tot can see the animals from low-lying or low-sitting carriages. Three climatic regions—the Rain Forest, Temperate Territory, and Polar Circle—form the focal points.

The Rain Forest is a veritable jungle, filled with the sounds and swirling mist of a roaring waterfall and the calls of tropical birds. Older children like the piranha aquarium and the ant nest, containing more than 100,000 leaf-cutter ants. A way-cool sight in the Temperate Territory is an island of Japanese snow monkeys in a lake with black-neck swans.

HEY, KIDS! Did you know the sea lion pool holds 100,000 gallons of water? Check out the glass panels for below-the-water views of their swimming antics, and try to get here at 11:30, 2, or 4. That's when they're fed. It's too much fun to miss.

KEEP IN MIND Special community events like National Pig Day, Migration Sensation, and Chill Out with the Polar Bears and Penguins are scheduled throughout the year, free with general admission. An interactive preschool series for children 3–5 with an adult is offered for a fee in various sessions throughout the year. Children's and family programs (some with charges) for youngsters 6 and up have included such favorites as Breakfast with the Birds, Snooze at the Zoo, Rainforest Retreat, and Spooky Species.

Central Park at 64th St. and 5th Ave.

$6 ages 13 and up, $1 children 3–12; some programs extra

Early Apr–late Oct, M–F 10–5, Sa–Su 10:30–5:30; late Oct–early Apr, daily 10–4:30

212/439–6500; www.centralparkzoo.org

All ages, children's zoo 6 and under

Speaking of cool, the Polar Circle contains some exhibits refrigerated to 34°F. Look for arctic foxes as well as the ever-popular penguins, puffins, and polar bears, whose natural habitats feature 10 viewing areas with above- and below-water views.

In the Tisch Children's Zoo, children can explore touch boxes, hear through huge rabbit ears, examine giant turtle shells and eggs, observe waterfowl from behind a child-size duck blind, and pet and feed many animals. Small animal sculptures moo, baa, or grunt when touched by little hands.

Costumed animal characters mingle with visitors, answering (and posing) questions. The Acorn Theater presents shows using puppets, costumed characters, music, and song to teach basic animal facts. Where else could you hear the "Metamorphosis Boogie" or participate in a Wildlife Workout? Something tells me it's all happening at the zoo.

EATS FOR KIDS Kids go wild for snacks at the zoo's indoor-outdoor **Cafe.** Central Park also has food stands near many entrances. You may recognize the pricey **Loeb Boathouse Cafe** (East Park Dr. and E. 72nd St., tel. 212/517–2233) from such movies as *Three Men and a Little Lady* and *When Harry Met Sally*; open March–September.

CHELSEA PIERS

Chelsea Piers has been called Manhattan's ultimate playground with spectacular views. After opening in 1995, it became the fourth-most-visited destination in the city (4.1 million visitors in 2000) in just five years, behind the Statue of Liberty and Ellis Island, the Metropolitan Museum of Art, and Madison Square Garden. This riverside recreation resort features bowling, basketball, soccer, in-line skating, swimming, sailing, kayaking, and rock climbing, and as incongruous as it sounds, your family can ice-skate in summer and play golf all winter, all on piers jutting into the Hudson River. The piers date back to 1910, part of nine piers that were a popular port of call for grand ocean liners. In 1994 the Chelsea Piers were restored and revitalized, and construction of the complex began.

The first thing to do is pick an activity. The Field House (between Piers 61 and 62, tel. 212/336–6500) is an 80,000-square-foot facility for gymnastics, team sports, basketball, soccer, and lacrosse. It contains four batting cages; dance studios; a martial arts mezzanine; a climbing wall designed for children, teens, and adult beginners; and the new Adventure

KEEP IN MIND At the 1¼-mile Waterside Promenade you can stroll, grab a bench, picnic at tables, or just relax and enjoy the spectacular Hudson River views. Free summer concerts and community events take place at the tip of Pier 62 at Pier Park. But if you decide to take a walk while your kids pursue other activities (younger children, of course, should be kept with you), plan to meet up later at a specific time at an agreed-upon, no-fail place. As this recreational mecca is a vast space, without a plan, you could be pacing the piers for hours.

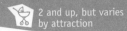
Center, an interactive play center for children 3 and under. Sky Rink (Pier 61, tel. 212/336–6100) is open 24/7, if you want to ice-skate at 3 AM.

AMF Chelsea Piers Bowl (between Piers 59 and 60, tel. 212/835–BOWL) is a 40-lane facility equipped with automatic scoring, bumper bowling for kids, and Xtreme Bowling, an evening bowling experience with black lights, Day-Glo pins, music, and fog machines. A Golf Center (Pier 59, tel. 212/336–6400) houses 52 heated and weather-protected hitting stalls on four levels with a computerized automatic ball tee-up system. You and your children can practice year-round or take lessons or classes from pros.

Like the city it's in, Chelsea Piers has something for everyone—adults, kids, New Yorkers, and visitors. If you lack equipment, you can rent or buy anything you need for an extraordinary visit to this 30-acre sports village.

HEY, KIDS! Check out one of the country's best vert ramps and street courses at the Skate Park at the Roller Rinks. Here you can safely "launch and grind" on over 20,000 square feet of ramps, pipes, flat rails, spines, fun boxes, and more.

EATS FOR KIDS **Chelsea Brewing Company** (Pier 59, tel. 212/336–6440), overlooking the marina, features casual riverside pub fare, including gourmet pizzas and pasta, indoors or out. For breakfast, lunch, or an evening meal, try the pastries and sandwiches at **Ruthy's Bakery & Café** (Main Plaza, Pier 62, tel. 212/336–6666), or take home a special-occasion cake for (you know) a special occasion. AMF Chelsea Piers Bowl features a full-service **café** and **lounge.** Or just picnic along the promenade.

CHILDREN'S MUSEUM OF MANHATTAN

One of the magical things about this museum is that there's always something new to see. Exhibits in the five floors of exhibition space change frequently. Grab your galoshes, unfold your umbrella, and get on board for some weather-related adventures with Ms. Frizzle if you're visiting Scholastic's Magic School Bus exhibit. You can follow the dream-adventure of Alice in Wonderland or bring literacy to life with Clifford the Big Red Dog and his friend Emily Elizabeth. The fun continues with a special Dr. Suess celebration, where your child's imagination can run wild.

Weather permitting from May through October, don't miss City Splash in the Sussman Environmental Center. This outdoor water-play area invites young visitors to explore the physical properties of water as they splash, pour, float, and play. (You may want to bring a change of clothes or towel in case of water-logged visitors.)

HEY, KIDS!

If you're 5 or older, be sure to sign up for a workshop in the Computer Lab, where you can use the latest digital imaging technology to create your own digital design to print and take home. You can also register for programs in the Creativity Lab, where you can explore the visual and performing arts, science, and literacy.

KEEP IN MIND Sing-alongs, Step into Story Adventures, art projects to make and take, and fun-for-the-whole-family performances by artists like Blue Man Group and the Time Square KIDZ are just a few of the programs offered throughout the year. Call ahead or check the Web site to see what's scheduled for the day you visit, or check the posted schedule of events as soon as you arrive. Then head first to the areas that pique your child's interest the most.

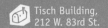 Tisch Building,
212 W. 83rd St.

 212/721-1234;
www.cmom.org

 $8 ages 1 and up

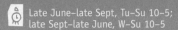 Late June–late Sept, Tu–Su 10–5;
late Sept–late June, W–Su 10–5

 Infants–10

Children 18 months to 4 years can climb, slide, paint, and sing in the intimate Early Childhood Center, a first museum-environment experience for kids. Art classes meet in the Russell Berrie Creativity Lab, also the site of a weekend multidisciplinary program for children 5 and older and a drop-in program for children 4 and younger (Thursday and Friday 10:30–4:30), which includes parachute play, multisensory exploration, music, art, and interactive storytelling. Story time for preschoolers takes place daily in the Helena Rubinstein Literacy Center. There's always something cooking, figuratively—sometimes even literally—at CMOM. See, Mom, it's worth missing a nap.

EATS FOR KIDS On weekdays, **EJ's Luncheonette** (447 Amsterdam Ave., tel. 212/873-3444) offers a 20% discount to Children's Museum of Manhattan members. Go for the blue-plate special or the skinless chicken. For a heaping helping of deli delights, visit **Artie's New York Delicatessen** (2290 Broadway, at 83rd St., tel. 212/579-5959).

CHILDREN'S MUSEUM OF THE ARTS

It's hard to know where to begin when entering this small SoHo museum, but somehow children manage. They set their own pace, find a space that interests them, and move on, often returning to their favorite workshop or exhibit. The focus here is hands-on art, based on the theory that children learn best by doing. And they do . . . and do. In 5,000 square feet of kid-comfortable space, they touch, create, and explore.

There's always something new here, as exhibitions rotate every three months, highlighting such themes as art from around the world or local book illustrators. Daily workshops follow the themes of color, line, and form and always include a painting project, sculpture activity, and work using found objects, reinforcing that art can and should be made out of everything.

Your children can draw on computers and then print their work, developing computer skills, artistic sensibilities, and hand-eye coordination without even realizing it. For older kids, the Artist's Studio features daily art projects involving problem solving and exploration

HEY, KIDS! Need to shake the sillies out? Jump into the Ball Pond, a carpeted area filled with large, brightly colored physioballs. The theory behind it is that the kinesthetic experience fosters motor-skill play, but you'll probably just think that it's a great place to get started in the museum. Thanks to the creative use of color, light, and texture, the surrounding area gives the illusion of being underwater. So dive right in!

 182 Lafayette St.

 212/274-0986;
www.cmany.org

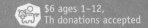 $6 ages 1–12,
Th donations accepted

 W and F–Su 12–5, Th 12–6

 1–10, Artist's Studio 6 and over,
Creative Play Area 4 and under

with a variety of art materials. It's not unusual to find artists from the community working side-by-side with the next artistic generation here. Meanwhile, younger visitors can enjoy the Creative Play Area, which includes an Art Station, where the art projects are designed for sensory stimulation. The Art House is a small two-story space with slide shows and costumes for pretend play.

Workshops in music, dance, theater, and puppetry instill confidence and foster skill mastery, open-ended exploration, and creativity. Check out the summer weeklong art camps and fall after-school programs for kids 6–12. Call ahead for info on daily music programs. Paintings, sculptures, and drawings from museum visitors, adult artists, and children from around the world are displayed throughout the museum. Along with changing items from the permanent collection, a number of special exhibitions and temporary displays are also hung throughout the year. Big things are created in a small space by little people with huge imaginations.

EATS FOR KIDS
In the mood for waffles any time of day? Visit the **Cupping Room Cafe** (359 W. Broadway, tel. 212/925–2898). Three-course, prix-fixe dinners (Monday and Tuesday) and weekend brunch are also treats. For a hip, moderately priced artist hangout, try **Jerry's** (101 Prince St., tel. 212/966–9464).

KEEP IN MIND The Children's Museum of the Arts conducts programs at the museum especially geared to special-needs children, their families, and schools. Another innovative series is the WEE Artists program (wondrous, experimenting, and exploring artists), held Wednesday–Friday 10–11:30 in summer and 10:45–noon the rest of the year. This drop-in program for 1- to 3-year-olds ($17 for a group/family of three) is a favorite with the toddler set.

CLAREMONT RIDING ACADEMY

Want to ride a horse, lease a horse, buy a horse, board a horse, or celebrate your birthday with one? You've come to the right place. This family-owned stable built in 1892—the oldest stable in continuous operation in the United States—is primarily a riding school. However, those who can demonstrate experience riding English may rent horses for an unaccompanied ride on the bridle paths of Central Park. The academy's horses are also hired for television, movies, and magazine and photo shoots. They have appeared in such movies as *Hair* and *Eyewitness* as well as Metropolitan Opera productions of *Aida*, *Carmen*, and *La Boheme*.

Group, semi-private, and private lessons in the year-round indoor riding arena are available by appointment. Up to 50 horses are also stabled here. If you've ever wondered what it would be like to own a horse, you can lease one here in a "try before you buy" arrangement.

KEEP IN MIND To gallop into the sunset in and around town, you can also take riding lessons at Pelham Bit Stable (tel. 718/885–0551), Bronx Equestrian Center (tel. 718/885–0551), Riverdale Equestrian Center (tel. 718/548–4848), and the New York City Riding Academy at Randalls Island (tel. 212/860–2986).

EATS FOR KIDS In the mood for fruit smoothies? Gallop over to **Cafe Con Leche** (424 Amsterdam Ave., near 81st St., tel. 212/595–7000; 726 Amsterdam Ave., near 96th St., tel. 212/678–7000). The garlic bread, ample portions of paella, and yellow rice are crowd pleasers. **Gabriela's** (685 Amsterdam Ave., at 93rd St., tel. 212/961–0574; 315 Amsterdam Ave., at 75th St., tel. 212/875–8532) has a popular kids' menu; the tacos and chicken are sure bets. The **Popover Café** (551 Amsterdam Ave., at 86th St., tel. 212/595–8555) is teddy bear heaven for brunch or delectable popovers any time.

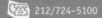 175 W. 89th St.

📠 212/724-5100

🐴 Lessons $50–$120, multisession discounts; horse hire $50 per hr.

 M–F 6:30 AM–10 PM, Sa–Su 6:30–5

🍼 6 and up

The monthly fee can be applied to the purchase price, should you wish to buy your steed at the end of your rental. A six-week Horse Care and Stable Management course is also offered, along with other special programs, including summer solstice, spring, and Christmas rides.

Claremont Riding Academy horse shows, limited to Claremont riders, are held in February and June. A summer riding camp includes full days with at least two lessons, hands-on horse care, and arts and crafts. Special theme days and parent visits round out this popular program. A winter camp is offered for two weeks in late December.

HEY, KIDS! Claremont Riding Academy provides a fabulously fun birthday party that includes pony rides, candy-in-the-haystack hunts, stable tours, lucky horseshoes, and romping in the ring. For an additional fee, pizza and carrot cake may be served in the blacksmith shop, and you can even be picked up or taken home in a horse-drawn carriage with family, friends, and your sack of birthday presents.

CLAY PIT PONDS STATE PARK PRESERVE

New York City's only state park preserve, these 260 natural acres near Staten Island's southwest shore were once the site of a clay-mining operation (hence the name). But to really tell its history, you have to go back to the Cretaceous period, nearly 70 million years ago, when sands and clays were deposited here. More recent glacial deposits, 12,000 years ago, add to the area's geological significance. Evidence of Leni Lenape Indians, European settlers, and the Free Blacks of Sandy Ground, who arrived from Maryland in the early 1800s, adds a cultural thread to the land's rich tapestry. But though the visitor center does have historical photos and a few artifacts, the main draw here is nature.

Established in 1977, the preserve harbors such diverse habitats as fields, sandy barrens, spring-fed streams, bogs and other freshwater wetlands, and woodlands, creating an oasis amid an urban area and enabling city dwellers to commune with nature. Each season paints a different natural backdrop. Throughout the year, wildflowers or their dried silhouettes can be seen along the trails. White wild carrot flowers and Queen Anne's lace frame

EATS FOR KIDS There are picnic tables behind preserve headquarters. German fare is on tap at **Killmeyer's** (4254 Arthur Kill Rd., tel. 718/984–1202). Weekend evenings and Sunday afternoons often bring an oompah band. The 1716 **Old Bermuda Inn** (2512 Arthur Kill Rd., tel. 718/948–7600) is a bit pricey for lunch and dinner, but the Sunday brunch is a good value.

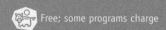
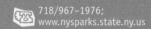

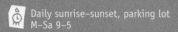

83 Nielsen Ave., Staten Island

Free; some programs charge

718/967-1976;
www.nysparks.state.ny.us

Daily sunrise–sunset, parking lot
M–Sa 9–5

2 and up

summer fields, folding up in winter to resemble tiny birds' nests. The wildflower garden behind headquarters is particularly colorful in spring, though some flowers blossom in late summer. Ask for a key to identify the garden's contents.

On your way to scope out the chicken coop, say hello to the resident goat, Maggie. She loves visitors and has been known to be very affectionate. Hiking and horseback riding are permitted on designated trails. Take the Abraham's Pond Trail (blue markers) to the Ellis Swamp Trail (yellow markers) for a 1-mile walk, or stay on the Abraham's Pond Trail the entire way, a ½-mile jaunt. The Green Trail meanders through a mature hardwood forest.

Free educational programming covers pond ecology, bird-watching, tree and wildflower identification, and organic gardening. Children's programs round out the experience.

KEEP IN MIND

Trails are for feet or hooves only, not tires or paws. Watch for nonpoisonous snakes—garter, black racer, and water snakes—not because they'd hurt us (they won't). They're only a threat to the insect and rodent populations they keep in check.

HEY, KIDS! Get a trail guide and look at its illustrations so you can identify the plants and animals you see on the preserve. Can you find a screech owl, box turtle, fence lizard, raccoon, or black-capped chickadee? In addition to helping put names to flora and fauna, the trail guide will alert you to landscape changes. Also look for structures, like steps or bridges, and trail markers, and remember not to disturb, destroy, or collect anything along your journey.

COLDEN CENTER FOR THE PERFORMING ARTS

Since 1961, the Colden Center for the Performing Arts at Queens College has been presenting world-class performing artists in the fields of music, dance, theater, jazz, popular entertainment, children's and family programming, and arts education. Performances can be seen at the Samuel J. and Ethel LeFrak Concert Hall, a 489-seat state-of-the-art recital hall with recording studio, or the Colden Auditorium, which seats 2,127 and has excellent acoustics and sight lines.

KidsClassics concerts are just what they sound like: a series of classical music concerts that involve children as active listeners. An eclectic musical menu followed by a hearty serving of audience participation captivates both young and old. Before the concerts, families can create their own musical instruments and add their artwork to the portable gallery. After the concerts, audience members are invited to stay to meet the artists.

EATS FOR KIDS For excellent, cheap noodle soup, try the Vietnamese restaurant **Pho Bang** (41–07 Kissena Blvd., tel. 718/939–5520). For cheap, fast, and hearty authentic Cantonese dishes, dine at the **Sweet-n-Tart Cafe** (136–11 38th Ave., tel. 718/661–3380).

KEEP IN MIND There's lots to see and do on campus besides performances. The Godwin-Ternbach Museum's collection comprises more than 3,500 artworks, and four major exhibitions are mounted annually. The Queens College Art Center's Benjamin S. Rosenthal Library exhibits modern and contemporary art. The Louis Armstrong Archives contain the great jazz pioneer's recordings, instruments, manuscripts, memorabilia, photographs, and scrapbooks. His home in Corona is also open to the public, with tours and special events in the Armstrong Garden. Log onto the Colden Center Web site for upcoming events and the Revelations section for kids.

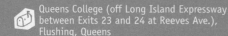 Queens College (off Long Island Expressway between Exits 23 and 24 at Reeves Ave.), Flushing, Queens

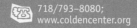 718/793–8080; www.coldencenter.org

 Varies by event

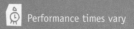 Performance times vary

 Varies by performance, KidsClassics 6–12

Family Theatre performances might include such universal favorites as the *Nutcracker* ballet, American Family Theatre's *Alice in Wonderland,* or the annual lunar New Year celebration, a Chinese or Korean music festival. Many events are ideal for all ages; others have age recommendations.

Besides the exceptional programming just for kids, selected all-age special events and individual performances in the fields of dance, music, and theater may also be of interest to your children. For example, an Asian art in performance series included such family events as the Peking Opera Festival, Japanese Taiko Drummers, and Tamara and the Shadow Theatre of Java. Budding instrumentalists may also be interested in the classical concert series.

HEY, KIDS! The KidsClassics "Classic Talk Program Guide" has really cool activities, puzzles, science experiments, and a musical "road map" to help you get the most out of these classical concerts. Rude Ralph can teach you about concert etiquette. Rap to the beat while you learn about percussion instruments and rhythm, and meet the musical members of the chamber orchestra—the instruments, that is. Try not to peek at the puzzle solutions and activity answers in the back of the book.

CONEY ISLAND

Developed as a seaside resort in the early 19th century, Coney Island became famous as a growing amusement center in the 1880s. By the 1950s, it became less popular as a resort destination but steadily grew as a residential area. Today summer crowds still flock to the boardwalk, the 3-mile beach, a huge amusement park (Astroland), and a seaside aquarium (*see* the New York Aquarium). Fishing on the pier, go-karts, a batting cage, and a sports center offering ice-skating and indoor sports round out the recreational opportunities. On warm and sunny days, you'll find a lively mix here, with summer weekends the busiest times. Apartment dwellers come to escape the stifling summer heat, teenagers come for the thrill rides, and families flock to Coney Island with kids in tow to rekindle a memory and to create new ones for the next generation.

Its glory days may be gone, but Astroland Amusement Park (1000 Surf Ave., tel. 718/372–0275) is still a family favorite. The wooden Cyclone roller coaster remains as popular today as it was when it first ran in 1927. A water flume, bumper cars, and other adult rides, as

HEY, KIDS! Consider this: the Wonder Wheel was built in 1920 with Bethlehem steel forged on-site. Standing 150 feet tall (half a football field), it has 16 swinging passenger cars and eight stationary cars and was declared a New York City landmark in 1989. The only time it stopped running was on July 13, 1977, during the infamous New York City blackout. To get the riders down to safety, the owners hand-cranked the huge wheel. Ready to ride?

well as 14 kiddie rides, are also on the amusement menu here. At Deno's Wonder Wheel Amusement Park (1025 Boardwalk, tel. 718/372–2592), 25 rides, two arcades, and an old-fashioned sweet shop are the main attractions. B&B Carousel (W. 11th St. and Surf Ave.) is also open year-round.

Lively traditional circus sideshows, complete with a fire-eater, sword swallower, snake charmer, and contortionist, are featured at Sideshows by the Seashore (W. 12th St. and Surf Ave.). Upstairs from the sideshows, you'll find the Coney Island Museum (open weekends noon to 5), which contains exhibits spotlighting historic Coney Island and related memorabilia. An extensive array of tourist information and literature is also available here.

Despite all its changes, Coney Island is still probably the closest you'll get to an old-fashioned seaside resort in New York.

EATS FOR KIDS
On the boardwalk you can grab a slice of pizza, an Italian ice, a large pretzel, or, better yet, a frank. After all, this is where Nathan's Famous made Coney Island hot dog history. If you're interested in restaurants, see the New York Aquarium.

KEEP IN MIND There are many individual (and sometimes questionable) ride operators up and down the boardwalk, so stick with Astroland, Deno's, and B&B Carousel. A real boon to the area and good news for sports fans is that baseball has returned to Brooklyn. The Brooklyn Cyclones, a minor league Class A affiliate of the New York Mets, takes to the field at the 6,500-seat KeySpan Park (Surf Ave. between W. 16th and W. 19th Sts.). Tickets are pleasantly affordable ($5–$12) and can be ordered online at www.brooklyncyclones.com or by phone at 718/507–TIXX.

ELLIS ISLAND

A symbol of America's immigrant experience, Ellis Island welcomed some 12 million people into the United States from 1892 until 1954. Today their descendants make up almost 40% of the U.S. population, as well as many of the visitors here. Should you choose to join those millions and set foot on this landmark, you can discover or rediscover this important part of American history.

The Ellis Island Immigrant Museum tells the remarkable stories of the immigrants who passed through these buildings. In three floors of self-guided exhibit and audio displays, it uses restored areas, educational facilities, and more than 2,000 artifacts—personal papers, jewelry, religious articles, and clothing—to tell tales of countless weary travelers. Enter through the first-floor Baggage Room, through piles of "all their worldly possessions," and view the video, which will help you plan your tour of the main building and the American Immigrant Wall of Honor. (Two award-winning films are shown on the first and second floors, and an interactive learning center is accessible by reservation only.)

EATS FOR KIDS You can eat at the convenient **food court** here, serving American and ethnic foods; pack a picnic; or, after you return, walk to the brick plaza behind 85 Broad Street for takeout from a small area restaurant. See Fraunces Tavern Museum and the South Street Seaport Museum.

GETTING THERE The Circle Line ferry sails from Battery Park, South Ferry, at Manhattan's southern tip, and includes a visit to the Statue of Liberty (*see #4*). The trip takes 15 minutes to Liberty Island, 15 minutes from there to Ellis Island, and 15 minutes back to Battery Park. It's good to catch the first boat in the morning to avoid long lines, unavoidable during the busiest times—weekends year-round and every day in summer. Refreshments and souvenirs are sold on board. Once on Ellis Island, you can stay as long as you like—until closing time.

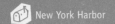

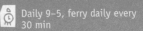

The next stop, Peopling of America, has 11 graphic displays chronicling four centuries of immigration. View the changing exhibits on the first floor before ascending to the Registry Room of the Great Hall. The hall, where immigrants were questioned and either granted or denied entry, has been restored. The cavernous space with soaring tiled arches seems to echo with the sounds of those hopeful souls.

See the remaining exhibits on the second and third floors before heading to the old kitchen and laundry building, offering a glimpse of what the island's structures looked like before restoration. Lastly, visit the American Immigrant Wall of Honor, where 600,000 immigrants' names are inscribed in steel along a promenade overlooking the Statue of Liberty. Families can pay to have a name added. Recognizable names include Miles Standish, Priscilla Alden, and Irving Berlin. It's the largest memorial wall of names in the world, fitting for a nation of immigrants.

HEY, KIDS! Most immigrants who arrived at Ellis Island were fleeing such hardships as poverty, religious persecution, and political unrest in their homelands. More than 1,500 firsthand accounts are preserved in the Oral History Library. You can sit at one of the listening stations and hear the voices of history. Do you have any ancestors who passed through the island? Try speaking to them or to someone who knows their story before your visit.

EMPIRE STATE BUILDING

One of the most-recognized and most-photographed buildings in the world, the art deco Empire State Building has graced the New York skyline since 1931. The 1,454-foot structure with a limestone and granite exterior was built in one year and 45 days for a total of $41 million. (Renovations over the last 15 years have cost an additional $100 million, more than double the original price.) Now a National Historic Landmark, it has been featured in hundreds of films viewed by millions of moviegoers. No wonder that first-time city visitors often make it their first sightseeing stop. More than 3.5 million people come here each year; the total since 1931 is over 125 million.

After you've purchased tickets on the concourse, one level below ground level, high-speed express elevators whisk you to the 86th-floor observatory in less than a minute. A temperature-controlled, glass-enclosed area offers panoramic views of the city, and you may also take in the sights from a surrounding open-air promenade. Try the on-site high-powered binoculars for a closer view.

HEY, KIDS! Want to go for a jog? In 1978 the first annual Empire State Building Run-up was held with the help of the New York Road Runners Club. Runners ran up 1,575 steps from the lobby to the 86th floor. Today the men's record is held by Paul Crake, who ran up the stairs in 9 minutes and 37 seconds in 2000. The women's record is held by Andrea Mayr of Austria, with a time of 12 minutes and 8 seconds set in 2004.

 350 5th Ave., at 34th St.

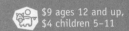 $9 ages 12 and up, $4 children 5–11

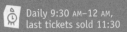 Daily 9:30 AM–12 AM, last tickets sold 11:30

 212/736–3100; www.esbnyc.com

 2 and up

Above the observatory are broadcast and transmission facilities serving New York City–area FM-radio and television stations, including new HDTV (high-definition television). The 102nd-floor observation deck has been closed to the public due to limited capacity.

On your way out, pause on the 34th Street side of the building to notice the series of eight towering illuminated panels depicting the Seven Wonders of the Ancient World. In 1955 the American Society of Civil Engineers designated the building the Eighth Wonder of the Modern World. Following the September 11 attack on the World Trade Center, the Empire State Building has implemented additional security measures.

KEEP IN MIND On a clear day you can see forever—at least about 80 miles and to five states: New York, New Jersey, Pennsylvania, Connecticut, and Massachusetts. Needless to say, plan to visit on a sunny day . . . or a cloudless night. Gazing down on the city that never sleeps reveals a sparkling tapestry.

EATS FOR KIDS Along with the observatory and gift shop, the 86th floor has a **snack bar**. The **Metro Grill** (45 W. 35th St., tel. 212/279–3535) is a great place to catch a bite to eat and a spectacular view of the Empire State Building. It's a bit pricey, but the steak and pastas are recommended. Got your sights set on pie in the sky? Try the ravioli pie or rigatoni pie at **Rosa's Pizza** (126 W. 32nd St., tel. 212/290–2315), right inside the Empire State Building. Also see restaurants in the Madison Square Garden listing.

FEDERAL HALL NATIONAL MEMORIAL

Built in 1703 to serve as New York's City Hall, Federal Hall became the first Capitol of the United States under the Constitution and is often considered the birthplace of our nation's government. On its steps stands a statue of George Washington created in 1883 by a relative of his, sculptor John Quincy Adams Ward. Washington was sworn in as the country's first president on this very site in 1789.

The original building was demolished in 1812, and the present structure was completed in 1842 and served as a U.S. Customs House. This Greek Revival building was modeled after the Parthenon, another symbol of democracy. Notice the impressive exterior's 16 Doric columns constructed of Tuckahoe marble, quarried in nearby Westchester County. Each column comprises five separate pieces, each weighing 10–12 tons. Walk through the front doors and you pass from Greece to Rome. The rotunda is based on the Pantheon and has 16 Corinthian columns.

EATS FOR KIDS Food and drink are not allowed here. **Burritoville** (20 John St., tel. 212/766–2020) serves cheap, healthy, and hefty burritos. **Cosi Sandwich Bar** (55 Broad St., tel. 212/344–5000) delights with tasty sandwiches and salads—worth the wait for the bread alone. Also, see the South Street Seaport Museum.

HEY, KIDS! Show me the money! When Federal Hall was a customs house (1842–62), millions in gold and silver were stored in basement vaults. No money—only exhibits—remain. Though people think of customs today mainly as a watchdog that prevents smuggling, in colonial times, it collected large fees from merchant vessels. In fact these fees were so big that they paid for setting up the new U.S. government; creating a navy; planning and building Washington, D.C.; constructing the military academy at West Point; and reducing the national debt to zero in 1835.

26 Wall St.

 M–F 9–5

 Free

 212/825-6888;
www.nps.gov/feha

 7 and up

Begin your visit with an eight-minute animated video on the history of majestic Federal Hall, from the trial of Peter Zenger to the inauguration of George Washington. An exhibit on the Zenger trial, a milestone in the establishment of freedom of the press, also includes an antique printing press. Can you imagine printing anything longer than a page on such a primitive press? Other key events that took place in the original building include the Stamp Act Congress of 1765, meetings of the Continental Congress, the enactment of the Northwest Ordinance, the adoption of the Bill of Rights, and the first meeting of the Congress of the United States.

Models of the original structure as City Hall and exhibits about the city and the Wall Street area are interesting, too. Look for historical memorabilia such as the bible used to swear in President Washington. Free guided tours cover the history of the buildings and interpretations of memorabilia and displays. Ranger-led talks describing this historic site are held on the hour from 10 to 4. It's like a social studies textbook come to life.

KEEP IN MIND In addition to finding information at Federal Hall about the site itself, you can also obtain brochures with self-guided themed walking tours of Lower Manhattan. While you're in the area, check out Castle Clinton, Fraunces Tavern Museum, Ellis Island, the Statue of Liberty, the National Museum of the American Indian (see listings), and the Staten Island Ferry. Kids can also take part in the Junior Ranger program and get a packet of goodies, including crossword puzzles, word searches, and even a Junior Ranger badge.

The Forbes Magazine Galleries showcase changing exhibitions from the magazine's collection of paintings, photographs, and autographs, but the big draw for kids is the personal collection of the late publisher Malcolm Forbes, on the ground floor, which includes toys and games and other unusual and sparkling items.

Items in the Toy Galleries include more than 500 toy boats and an army of 10,000 toy soldiers engaged in imaginative displays. A special concave viewing window lets children enter the whimsical childhood room depicted in Robert Louis Stevenson's poem, "The Land of Counterpane." Also ongoing here is a display of original handcrafted versions of the board game Monopoly and the game that inspired it, the Landlord's Game. A 1913 English version called the Br'er Fox an' Br'er Rabbit game is also exhibited. But Forbes's noted collection goes far beyond toys to include historical documents and memorabilia. Thomas Jefferson's bottle of 1787 Château Lafite, Abraham Lincoln's stovepipe hat, and various presidential papers reveal the personalities and problems of many U.S. presidents. Four miniature

KEEP IN MIND For children (and adults) truly smitten by what they see, here are a few publications to check out: *Forbes Galleries* covers collection highlights and has an introduction from the collector himself. *A Lifetime of Collecting* is Forbes's autobiography, containing 572 photographs showcasing many of his treasures. *Toy Boats* offers a pictorial history of the rare tin, cast-iron, and wooden boats, dating from 1870 to 1955, in the Forbes collection.

 Forbes Building, 62 5th Ave., at 12th St.

 Free

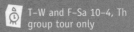 T–W and F–Sa 10–4, Th group tour only

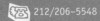 212/206–5548

 4 and up

rooms—Washington's headquarters at the Battle of Yorktown, John Adams's kitchen law office in Massachusetts, Ulysses S. Grant's dining room, and Jefferson's bedroom and study at Monticello—forge snapshots of American history.

If your youngsters find history dull, they might find the trophies, medals, and awards in the Mortality of Immortality exhibit shinier and more interesting. As Forbes wrote, "The trophy memorabilia are humbling reminders that objects marking great occasions or victories cannot stop the march of time and that, as the pharaohs learned, you can't take the stuff with you." These collections can't help but make you think that, wealth and power notwithstanding, Forbes had a lot of kid in him.

HEY, KIDS! Do you collect anything? When did you start? Don't worry if your collection is a little smaller than Forbes's; he had a whole lifetime and a lot of money to spend. To have even more fun, visit the library to learn more about your treasures and how to catalog them.

EATS FOR KIDS In the mood for sandwiches and pasta from every corner of the United States? Try **America** (9 E. 18th St., tel. 212/505–2110). For big, big, big burritos at low, low, low prices, try **Benny's Burritos** (113 Greenwich Ave., tel. 212/727–0584). **NoHo Star** (330 Lafayette St., tel. 212/925–0070) offers American as well as Chinese fare. Children will probably opt for hamburgers and french fries, omelets, or pancakes, while parents can be a bit more adventurous.

FRAUNCES TAVERN MUSEUM

43

The fact that this museum is open on July 4 and Washington's birthday (though closed on other holidays) should immediately tell you something about it. Fraunces Tavern—a large brick house built by Etienne Delancey in 1719 on the city's first landfill—was a meeting place for the Sons of Liberty as well as the site where George Washington said farewell to his loyal officers at the Revolution's end. The oldest building left in Manhattan today, it serves as New York's museum of Colonial, Revolutionary, and early republic history.

The building got its name from tavern-keeper Samuel Fraunces, who ran one of the finest dining and drinking establishments in colonial New York. Colonial governor George Clinton threw a huge gala here on Evacuation Day, when the last British soldiers left American soil at the end of the Revolutionary War. The tavern building was also where the Departments of War, State, and Treasury were housed when New York was the first capital of the United States.

HEY, KIDS!
Each month you can take part in Family Saturday Workshops, designed for kids of all abilities and free with museum admission. Recent programs have included Stars and Stripes Forever, Rag Rugs, Game Day, Smells of the Holidays, and Corn Husk Dolls.

EATS FOR KIDS Except for the price, which is more expensive than the neighborhood's many delis, coffee shops, and sandwich places, not to mention the 18th century, **Fraunces Tavern** (tel. 212/968-1776), part of the complex that includes the museum, is the place to go back in time while dining. The best bet is the prix-fixe menu ($20.05), which includes appetizer, entrée, and a delicious dessert. The bar has a slightly less expensive menu with hamburgers and other kid-friendly food. The huge Revolutionary War mural should interest most young diners. The tavern is open for lunch and dinner Monday–Saturday. Also see the South Street Seaport Museum.

54 Pearl St.

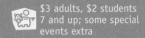 $3 adults, $2 students 7 and up; some special events extra

 T–Sa 10–5

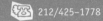 212/425-1778

 6 and up

Start at the Visitor Orientation Exhibition, which illustrates the history of the tavern and early New York. From there, visit the Long Room, site of Washington's famous farewell address and now a re-created 18th-century public tavern room. The Clinton Room, named for George Clinton, the first American-born governor of New York, represents an early 19th-century private dining room. A Flash of Color: Early American Flags and Standards highlights national symbols from different periods throughout American history. Included are regimental flags from the Revolution, flags of French troops, and naval banners. Changing exhibitions also shed light on Colonial times.

On special holidays—Washington's birthday, Flag Day, and Independence Day—Fraunces Tavern Museum holds open houses with free admission to the day's festivities.

KEEP IN MIND Walking tours, tea parties, 18th-century music and dance programs, and evening and lunchtime lectures are just some of the public programs held at the Fraunces Tavern Museum that can enrich your museum experience. But it's a good idea to call the museum's recorded information line ahead of time to determine which of the upcoming programs are appropriate for the ages in your family.

In the heart of Staten Island, this beautiful 100-acre park may be one of the city's best-kept secrets. The village contains 28 preserved historic buildings and a few reconstructions that interpret three centuries of Staten Island's daily life and culture. Ten buildings are on their original sites; the others were moved from elsewhere on Staten Island. Currently 12 buildings are open to the public.

The village of Richmond began in the 1690s as a crossroads settlement among scattered farms. The Congregation of the Reformed Dutch Church built a combined religious meeting house, school, and residence for its lay minister and teacher around 1695. By 1730, Richmond had become the island's principal political center, and throughout the 18th century the village continued to increase in importance, acquiring a jail, courthouse, churches, taverns, and shops.

Few barricades separate visitors from the places where people once worked and lived. Each room, whether equipped with the tools of a trade or filled with the aroma of something

KEEP IN MIND If you're planning a visit, call to see if any special family events (reservations required for some) are coming up. A sampling includes Halloween in Richmond Town, Old Home Day/Harvest Festival, Christmas in Richmond Town, an Independence Day Celebration, Pumpkin Picking at the Decker Farm, and a historic military Encampment Weekend. The Richmond County Fair also takes place here, combining traditional events with modern pastimes.

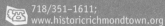 441 Clarke Ave., Staten Island

 $5 adults, $3.50 children 6–18 and students; some special events extra

718/351–1611;
www.historicrichmondtown.org

July–Aug, W–Sa 10–5, Su 1–5; Sept–June, W–Su 1–5

3 and up

baking, will take you back in time. Begin at the 1837 Third County Courthouse Visitor Center to get a visitor's guide to points of interest. The Historical Museum is in the former County Clerk's Office. The Voorlezer's House is Richmond's oldest building on its original site as well as the country's oldest elementary schoolhouse. Your children may chuckle at the outhouse and marvel at demonstrations of printing, tinsmithing, and other trades performed by artisans in period costumes. Children may be asked to lend a hand in the Basketmaker's House or help with another chore. When demonstrations aren't happening, a guide is present to give an overview of the setting and answer questions.

Special events are offered at various times, but you can count on traditional folk and ethnic music—showcased in the Tavern Concert Series—on Saturday evenings, January–April. The 19th-century Guyon Tavern is warmed by a woodstove and lit by candles to add to the atmosphere.

HEY, KIDS! Some of the best-loved toys from the 1840s to the present are displayed in the Historical Museum in TOYS! Can you recognize the toys and how children played with them? Imagine what childhood, family life, and work were like in the days of those toys.

EATS FOR KIDS **The Parsonage** (74 Arthur Kill Rd., tel. 718/351–7879) serves some history with your meal. It was the official residence of the Reformed Dutch Church minister (1855–75). **M. Bennett Refreshments** is open seasonally in the former cellar bakery in the Greek Revival–style Bennett House. The popular summertime traditional dinner, held once a year, includes an Early American menu prepared over open fires with music, games, and century-old toasts (reservations required). A picnic area is just east of the visitor center.

INTREPID SEA AIR SPACE MUSEUM

41

Not your typical museum, the Intrepid Sea Air Space Museum is a unique part of the landscape—make that seascape—of Manhattan's west side. The U.S.S. *Intrepid,* a 40,000-ton, 900-foot-long aircraft carrier, launched in 1943, was once scheduled to be scrapped after 31 years of military service. However, in 1982, after a successful campaign to save it, this historic ship was put into different service—as a museum.

Your children don't have to know history to sense adventure when standing among dozens of vintage and modern aircraft parked wing to wing on the carrier's flight deck, or when hearing a former crew member tell stories of this noble vessel. Video kiosks display the ship's heroic past, which includes five kamikaze strikes, one torpedo attack, and seven bombs. After each repair, the ship returned to active duty, earning her a reputation as the "Ghost Ship."

But there are other craft here, too. Don't miss the U.S.S. *Growler,* the only intact strategic missile submarine open to the public. Since 1989, this 3,000-ton, 317-foot-long sub

HEY, KIDS!

Fly your own jet mission aboard a navy flight simulator. Take off in your F-18 Hornet jet fighter. Dodge enemy tanks, missiles, and hostile aircraft as you attempt to return unharmed. Admission is $10 in addition to museum entry for the G-Force Encounter and $8 for the new 4-D Experience ride.

EATS FOR KIDS When was the last time you dined on a 900-foot-long aircraft carrier? The crew's **mess** has been refurbished so you can eat your meals here, just like the crew did. Bring your own if you like. A variety of sandwiches, snacks, and drinks can also be purchased on board. A **McDonald's** is located in the Visitor's Center area, near the gift shop.

Pier 86, W. 46th St. and 12th Ave.

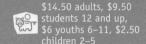 $14.50 adults, $9.50 students 12 and up, $6 youths 6–11, $2.50 children 2–5

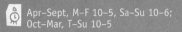 Apr–Sept, M–F 10–5, Sa–Su 10–6; Oct–Mar, T–Su 10–5

 212/245-0072; www.intrepidmuseum.org

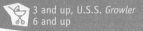 3 and up, U.S.S. *Growler* 6 and up

has offered a firsthand look at life on board as well as the once "top-secret" command post. You can see the Lockheed A-12 Blackbird, the world's ultimate spy plane. Along with the Blackbird, the *Intrepid*'s aircraft collection includes WWII fighters, supersonic jets, wood and canvas biplanes, and an F-16 Air Force Falcon, just to name a few. Where else can you climb inside a replica of a war submarine and an Intruder cockpit?

The film *Intrepid Wings* is shown in the new Allison and Howard Lutnick Theater, and special events include Tugboat Fest and Air Force, N.Y. Fire Department, and N.Y. Police Department weekends. Also here is Felix DeWeldon's original sculpture of the Iwo Jima Memorial, which portrays five marines and a sailor raising a U.S. flag during WWII. (The more famous, larger version is on display at Arlington National Cemetery.) Like the rest of the exhibits at this museum, it's a tribute to the people and vessels who have served our country at sea.

KEEP IN MIND Prepare your kids ahead of time for the possible wait to tour the U.S.S. *Growler*. Access is limited to only 15 people at a time, and very young children are not allowed aboard. And, if you have a friend or relative who served or serves aboard ship, you might want to bring him or her along; someone with firsthand experiences can certainly enhance your children's experience of this museum.

JEWISH MUSEUM

Nestled in the elegant 1908 Warburg Mansion on the city's Museum Mile, the Jewish Museum chronicles 4,000 years of Jewish culture through art. The permanent exhibition, called "Culture and Continuity, the Jewish Journey," occupies 17 galleries on the third and fourth floors. A family audio guide (free), for ages 5 and up, and an activity book ($18 in the museum's shop) guide you through this core exhibit. Art, artifacts, and media installations examine both perpetual and changing aspects of the Jewish cultural experience. Young visitors tend to find the re-creation of an ancient synagogue of interest, whereas older children enjoy television and radio programs from the museum's broadcast archive as well as a film on Jewish rituals in a gallery filled with ceremonial objects.

In addition, many areas and programs at the Jewish Museum are specifically devoted to children. The fourth-floor Children's Gallery has changing exhibitions for young visitors, and each always includes interactive components for inquiring minds and busy hands. On Sunday you can drop into the Family Activity Center and participate in a hands-on crafts

EATS FOR KIDS Lunch, snacks, and a light dinner are available at the museum's **Cafe Weissman.** You can't go wrong at the **Barking Dog Luncheonette** (1678 3rd Ave., tel. 212/831–1800), offering breakfast, lunch, dinner, brunch, and a drinking fountain just for canines, in case you've brought your pooch (though it's not allowed inside). Try a burger on focaccia bread, the marvelous meat loaf, or a yogurt sundae with granola topping. For homestyle, wholesome food, not to mention a great Sunday brunch, try **Sarabeth's** (Hotel Wales, 1295 Madison Ave., tel. 212/410–7335). Sample the raison scones, sticky buns, or pumpkin waffles.

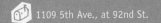 1109 5th Ave., at 92nd St.

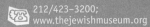 212/423-3200;
www.thejewishmuseum.org

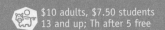 $10 adults, $7.50 students
13 and up; Th after 5 free

 Su–W 11–5:45, Th 11–8, Fr 11–3;
Family Activity Center Su 1–4;
story time Su 1:30

 2 and up

workshop for a nominal materials fee; you can also listen to a free ½-hour story time or take part in free Children's Gallery talks, informal interactive minitours of the core exhibit that meet on the third floor. The museum's first two floors contain temporary exhibits that are more often of interest to adults, and there are two gift shops, one in the museum and one next door in a brownstone.

Other family programs include Stories and Songs for Tots, Art in the Afternoon, and holiday craft and activity workshops. Many events are free; others have a small fee. Family concerts and special performances by well-known artists, like Marc Weiner from *Weinerville*, are scheduled throughout the year. Just check with the museum by phone or on its Web site to see if something's happening that would interest your family.

HEY, KIDS! Look for Ari (that means "lion" in Hebrew) throughout the museum. Ari's picture marks fun experiences of particular interest to young museum visitors. And don't forget to say "shalom," which means "hello" and "good-bye" as well as "peace" in Hebrew.

KEEP IN MIND If your family finds it hard to come up with something to do on Christmas, consider coming here. Unless December 25 falls on a Saturday, the museum hosts a special Family Day with a huge array of family activities, including a colossal art workshop in the auditorium, live music, and children's video screenings. How many museums do you know of that are open on Christmas?

JONES BEACH STATE PARK

New York State's most renowned state park opened in 1929 and hosted 1½ million visitors its first year. Sunday traffic jams on the (then) Wantagh Causeway started soon after, and not much has changed since. Today the Wantagh Parkway still jams up on weekends as families flock to the beach's eight Atlantic Ocean bathing areas and Zachs Bay from points even farther than New York City, 33 miles away.

The park comprises 2,413 acres with 6½ miles of beach frontage and ½ mile of bay frontage. East and West bathhouses feature Olympic-size pools, diving areas, wading pools, lockers, and showers. A 2-mile boardwalk is popular with young and old, and there are shuffleboard courts, paddle tennis, softball fields, volleyball, miniature golf, a fitness course, basketball, dancing nightly at the band shell, concerts, and special events. Surfing is permitted at the West End 2 area from the Monday after Thanksgiving through Labor Day, so surfer-free families may wish to avoid this crowd. With really young children, head to Zachs Bay, a gentle bathing area (don't even think about waves). Moms and dads have been dutifully

GETTING THERE By train, take the LIRR to Freeport or Wantagh, where buses (tel. 516/ 228–4000) connect to the beach. By car, take the Northern or Southern state parkways or LIE east to the Meadowbrook or Wantagh parkways south to the park.

EATS FOR KIDS Part of the fun of the beach is crunching that sand in your peanut butter sandwich. But for those who choose not to cart a 10-ton cooler across the beach, **refreshment stands** dispense drinks, cool desserts, hot dogs, and snacks. National chains, including **Nathan's** (nine locations), **Pizza Hut,** and **Friendly's** (nine locations including an ice cream parlor/restaurant above the West Bathhouse), can be found all along the boardwalk and at other concessions. Barbecue and picnic areas are also abundant.

 Ocean Dr., Wantagh

 $8 per car; some attractions extra

 Daily sunrise–12 AM

 516/785–1600, 516/221–1000 Jones Beach Theatre; www.nysparks.com

9 mth and up

depositing tots 10 yards from the family blanket in a puddle of water for years, and it's still a great first ocean experience.

The Tommy Hilfiger Jones Beach Theatre, at Zachs Bay, offers a sensational summer concert schedule with seating for 14,000. A 104-foot-wide stage with a 76-foot revolving center has an underwater tunnel leading from shore to stage and underground elevators for supplies and scenery.

Surf fishing areas, docks, a boat basin, and the bait station welcome anglers. The Theodore Roosevelt Nature Center (West End 1) is open Wednesday–Sunday Memorial Day–Labor Day and weekends the rest of the year. An activity center, the Discovery Bone Cove, an environmental boardwalk, lectures, hikes, and workshops round out the program. Whether you want to play, sunbathe, or swim, Jones Beach is ideal.

HEY, KIDS! As you approach the beach by bus or by car, be on the lookout for the Jones Beach Tower, a familiar landmark modeled after the campanile of St. Mark's Cathedral in Venice. It's 231 feet high and made of brick and stone, housing a 315,000-gallon water tank. Believe it or not, this tower provides all the water for the entire park. So if you're about to ask, "Are we there yet?" just look for the Jones Beach Tower instead.

LIBERTY SCIENCE CENTER

Many consider this one of the nation's top 10 science centers. The first thing to wow your children (and you) is the 700-pound Hoberman Sphere, which expands and contracts repeatedly in the atrium. It's mesmerizing to watch it seemingly explode into the huge space. But don't linger too long, or you miss all the fun on the three themed floors.

On the Environment Floor, climb across a 20-foot rock wall full of fossils or check out sea urchins and spider crabs in the Touch Tank. Get your hands dirty at the Stream Table, and befriend insects, snakes, and reptiles in the Green House Discovery Room.

A popular Health Floor destination for the 7-and-up crowd is the Touch Tunnel. Crawl through this 100-foot black tube with only touch to guide you. Close by, enter the world of optical illusion in the Perception Maze. At the medical imaging station, you can use MRI and CT scans to explore the human body, and don't forget to climb into the ambulance, the center's very first exhibit.

GETTING THERE Don't let the New Jersey location scare you; driving takes less than 30 minutes. Just get to New Jersey Turnpike exit 14B, bear left after the tollbooth, and follow signs. Or take the PATH to the Exchange Place or Pavonia/Newport station and transfer to the sleek Hudson–Bergen Light Rail toward 22nd Street or West Side Avenue for a 15-minute ride to Liberty State Park. Then follow the science experiments embedded in the sidewalk. You can also take the NY Waterway ferry (*see #18*) from the World Financial Center to Jersey City's Colgate Center and hop on the light rail (800/626–RIDE; www.njtransit.com).

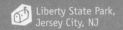 Liberty State Park,
Jersey City, NJ

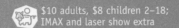 $10 adults, $8 children 2–18;
IMAX and laser show extra

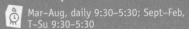 Mar–Aug, daily 9:30–5:30; Sept–Feb,
T–Su 9:30–5:30

201/200–1000;
www.lsc.org

 2 and up

Next comes the Invention Floor. In the virtual sports stadium, kids can challenge a computer or a friend to basketball, volleyball, snowboarding, or undersea diving. Visit Invention Central to discover the inventor inside you.

Each exhibit floor has a discovery room, where staff members present hands-on activities, and a science demonstration stage, where informative and entertaining shows take place. Don't miss a 3-D laser journey in the Joseph D. Williams Science Theater or the latest IMAX film in the nation's largest IMAX dome theater—six stories high. Many of the more than 250 interactive exhibits may be too complex for preschoolers, but each floor has some activities for them. In late 2005, the museum will begin a major expansion, which will nearly double its size. During construction you can visit the center's temporary quarters in the historic Central Railroad of New Jersey Terminal in Liberty State Park, on the Hudson River.

HEY, KIDS! At the science center's Web site, you can meet Betty Bug—a.k.a. Dr. Betty Faber, staff scientist and entomologist. She'll show you some cool stuff to see and do. It's the "creepiest" Web site you'll ever log on to.

EATS FOR KIDS Check out the **Laser Lights Cafe,** on the main floor, for reasonably priced entrées that appeal to both young and old. Choose from pizza, burgers and fries, franks, chili with cheese, sandwiches, and salads. This cafeteria makes for a nice break in a full day and a good place to plan your strategy for the afternoon.

LOWER EAST SIDE TENEMENT MUSEUM

37

Chronicling a variety of immigrant and migrant experiences in Manhattan's Lower East Side, this urban living-history experience comprises a series of guided tours of an 1863 tenement building (the first tenement declared a National Historic Landmark) and its neighborhood. The museum is only open through guided tours, which start at the Visitors Center. Video presentations tell the history of the building and neighborhood, and feature interviews with residents past and present.

The one-hour "Confino Family Apartment" tour focuses on this Sephardic-Jewish family in 1916. "Getting By: Weathering the Great Depressions of 1873 and 1929" is a one-hour visit to the apartments of the Gumpertz family from Germany and the Baldizzi family from Italy. "Piecing It Together" is a one-hour tour of the apartments of the Levines, who ran a garment factory from their parlor, and the Rogarshevsky family from Lithuania. The "Neighborhood Walking Tour" is a 1½-hour stroll (probably too much for young

HEY, KIDS!

The Confino apartment tour is a hands-on experience. A costumed guide will welcome you as if you're a newly arrived immigrant. Perhaps Mom and Dad can fox trot to the music on the wind-up Victrola. If you try hard, maybe you can imagine a child's life here in 1916.

EATS FOR KIDS Ethnic eateries abound. Have a knish or potato latkes (pancakes) at **Yonah Schimmel's Knishery** (137 E. Houston St., tel. 212/477–2858), a Lower East Side institution that began from a pushcart. For dim sum or veggie dumplings, try **20 Mott Street** (20 Mott St., tel. 212/964–0380). Hungry for a family favorite? Try **Grilled Cheese NYC** (168 Ludlow St., tel. 212/982–6600) for mom's rendition or gourmet combos of this American classic.

 Visitors Center, 90 Orchard St., at Broome St.; tenement, 97 Orchard St.

 212/431–0233; www.tenement.org

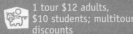 1 tour $12 adults, $10 students; multitour discounts

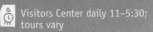 Visitors Center daily 11–5:30; tours vary

 8 and up

children) through the Lower East Side. Any of these walks back in time reveal families' daily struggle to survive.

Round-table discussions on mostly adult topics are scheduled year-round as are children's and family programs. The Tenement Theatre at John Schneider's Saloon, in the tenement's basement, stages plays about the modern-day immigrant experience. Storefront Windows, a public art display, reflects the many people who call this neighborhood home.

If you have a relative or friend who was an immigrant on the Lower East Side, or who knows stories of those days, you might want to invite that person along to provide a first- or second-hand perspective. Or take a decidedly more modern (virtual) tour by logging onto the museum's Web site. However you visit, your children will probably gain an appreciation for New York's present by catching a glimpse of its past.

KEEP IN MIND Tour tickets are available on a first-come, first-served basis, and they sell out quickly, as groups are limited to 15. Tickets for weekday tours and programs may be purchased in advance by credit card by calling 800/965–4827 or through www.ticketweb.com (multitour discounts are not available through this Web site). Sunday at the museum is especially crowded, but if you come by car, you can enjoy four hours of free parking at a lot on Broome Street, between Norfolk and Suffolk streets, courtesy of the Lower East Side Business Improvement District.

MADAME TUSSAUD'S WAX MUSEUM

Leave your autograph book at home, but grab your camera and get up close and personal with your favorite celebrities at Madame Tussaud's Wax Museum. Though Madame Tussaud's has been entertaining Europeans with its signature wax portraits for more than 200 years, this $50 million, 85,000-square-foot, five-story New York City showplace is relatively new. More than 200 uncannily lifelike wax portraits are featured in six themed, interactive exhibits. You can take photographs of your family with a virtual who's who of movies, music, sports, and television, as well as world leaders and other influential historical personalities.

The Opening Night Party, in a baroque Italian garden, lets you mingle with the New York A-list while waiting for the latest Broadway reviews to be posted. Look for Samuel L. Jackson, John Travolta, Oprah Winfrey, Hugh Grant, Bette Midler, Meryl Streep, and Nicolas Cage, among others, sharing the latest gossip. Go Behind the Scenes, with Al Roker, uses multimedia displays to demonstrate the often painstaking methods used to create a wax portrait. Follow Roker from his first sitting to the final touch-up of hair and makeup.

EATS FOR KIDS Hungry for a quick snack? The museum has a **snack bar** with popcorn, pretzels, ice cream, and soft drinks. Directly across the street, **Chevys** (243 W. 42nd St., tel. 212/302–4010) has great Tex-Mex food and an extensive menu for kids and adults that's not a lot of dough. Speaking of which, the kids' crayons come in a mound of dough, which isn't how Madame Tussaud got her start in sculpting. In the same building but two doors down from the wax museum, the **42nd Street Eatery** is a food court with fare from popular chains like **Applebee's** and **Cinnabon.**

 234 W. 42nd St.

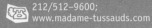 $27.99 ages 13 and up, $23.99 children 4–12; film $2 extra

 M–Th 10–6, F–Su 10–8

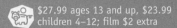 212/512–9600; www.madame-tussauds.com

 5 and up

In the Gallery you'll come face-to-face with American presidents and great leaders who've made a difference. Can you find the Dalai Lama, Maya Angelou, John F. Kennedy, Albert Einstein, Martin Luther King, Jr., and Diana, Princess of Wales? Move on to Popular Culture, where you'll meet trendsetters and celebrities. Babe Ruth, the Beatles, Marilyn Monroe, Neil Armstrong, Bill Gates, and Frank Sinatra are all presented in decade-specific vignettes.

The film *New York, New York* is a magical midnight ride via virtual Hansom cab through major events in New York City's illustrious history. Young children (and some adults) may find it a bit uncomfortable to look up at the domed ceiling screen while leaning on rails (no seats here). Is it any wonder that nearly 12 million guests visit Madame Tussaud's sites around the world each year?

HEY, KIDS! It takes six months and approximately $75,000 to create a wax figure, including five weeks alone for each head, since hair strands are inserted individually. Once on exhibit, each wax portrait is inspected and groomed daily, and its hair is washed and makeup retouched regularly.

KEEP IN MIND If you have young or extremely sensitive children, do not—repeat, do not—enter Madame Tussaud's Story. In an 18th-century setting, this exhibit chronicles the 200-year history of Madame Tussaud and her work and depicts scenes from the French Revolution as well as the beheading of Marie Antoinette and Napoleon's lover Josephine in prison. The disturbingly graphic display, sounds of war, and dark, depressing scenery are extremely alarming to youngsters. (Trust me on this one.)

MADISON SQUARE GARDEN

Sitting on top of Penn Station and spanning nearly 1 million square feet in the heart of New York City, this is perhaps the world's most famous arena. Generations of New Yorkers can fondly remember coming to various incarnations of "the Garden" to see a variety of sports, from boxing to basketball, as well as other types of performances. Today's Madison Square Garden traces its beginnings to the 1874 Great Roman Hippodrome, built by showman P. T. Barnum. In 1877 it was taken over by bandmaster Patrick Gilmore and renamed Gilmore's Garden. In 1879 Cornelius Vanderbilt's son, William, renamed the complex Madison Square Garden, and so its descendant—which opened in 1968 and was fully renovated in 1991—is known today.

The main arena seats 20,000 and is the spring site of performances by Ringling Bros. and Barnum & Bailey Circus. It's also home to the New York Knicks and New York Liberty basketball teams, New York Rangers hockey team, and events ranging from tennis tournaments to boxing bouts, and from horse shows to track meets. In 1877 Gilmore's Garden played

HEY, KIDS!
The Walk of Fame showcases names—from Elton John to Billie Jean King to Gunther Gebel-Williams—representing over a century of memorable sports and entertainment. In 1992 the first 25 members, chosen from more than 240 nominees, were inducted. See how many famous people you can identify.

EATS FOR KIDS You can get a deli sandwich at **Ben's Kosher Delicatessen** (209 W. 38th St., tel. 212/398–2367) or dunk a donut at **Krispy Kreme** (2 Penn Plaza, 33rd St. on Amtrak level, tel. 212/947–7175). Head to Macy's and **Emack & Bolio's** (151 W. 34th St., 4th fl., tel. 212/494–5853) for ice cream and yogurt in heavenly flavors. In addition to memorabilia discounts, your tour ticket stub is good for 10% off weekday lunch and during Knicks, Rangers, and Liberty games at the Garden sports restaurant, **Play by Play** (4 Penn Plaza, tel. 212/465–5888). For other choices, check out Penn Station's lower concourse.

 7th Ave. between 31st and 33rd Sts.

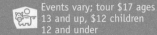 Events vary; tour $17 ages 13 and up, $12 children 12 and under

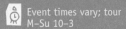 Event times vary; tour M–Su 10–3

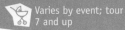 212/465–MSG1, 212/465–5800 tours; www.thegarden.com

Varies by event; tour 7 and up

host to the first annual N.Y. Bench Show, now famous as the Westminster Kennel Club Dog Show. Various ice shows and other children's fare are offered throughout the year. The 5,600-seat Theater at Madison Square Garden also hosts children's shows, such as *Sesame Street Live* and *A Christmas Carol*, as well as special events like the NFL draft.

Your family can also take the one-hour All Access Tour, which starts in the box office lobby under the distinctive Bulova Clock and continues through the arena, the theater's backstage, luxurious Garden suites, the historic Walk of Fame, Great Moments Photo Display, and locker rooms of the Knicks, Rangers, and Liberty. Stand courtside on the Knicks floor, get behind the glass on the Rangers ice, and learn how the basketball court becomes a hockey rink. You never know whom you might see. Rock stars practicing for concerts, movie and TV stars in theatrical performances, and pro athletes have been known to pose for pictures. The tour is an exciting add-on if you're planning to attend a sporting event here, especially if your children are true sports fans.

GETTING THERE It's "easy" to drive here, but beware of traffic. By subway, take the 1, 2, 3, or 9 (7th Avenue line) or the A, C, or E (8th Avenue line) to Penn Station or the B, D, F, N, Q, R, or PATH trains to 34th Street and 6th Avenue. The LIRR, NJ Transit, and Amtrak all stop in Penn Station. From Grand Central, take the S subway shuttle to Times Square and then a 7th Avenue subway. By bus, take the M4 or M10 here or any north–south bus to 34th Street and transfer to the M34 or M16 crosstown.

At 2 million square feet, the Met, as it's known, is the largest art museum in the Western Hemisphere. Its permanent collection houses nearly 2 million works of art from all over the world, including objects from the Paleolithic era to modern times. If you spent a minute looking at each object here without taking a break, it would take more than four years to see it all. So start small. Pick two to four areas to explore and plan to return. Free lectures and walking tours covering various parts of the museum are offered, and the museum's Family Audio Guide, ideal for children 6–12, includes commentary about more than 100 works of art.

Certain areas of the Met are particularly fascinating to children, and yours will no doubt enjoy the Costume Institute, on the ground floor, as well as the musical instruments, on the second floor by the American Wing's courtyard. Check out the baseball cards in the first-floor American Wing side gallery. Be sure to visit the popular Arms and Armor Hall, on the first floor, and the Egyptian Galleries. Check out the mummies and the Temple of

EATS FOR KIDS All museum restaurants, including the **American Wing Café** and **Great Hall Balcony Bar,** welcome children, but the **cafeteria** is especially family friendly. It has booster seats, high chairs, and special meals for kids 12 and under ($4.95) that come with fruit and milk or juice in a cool 3-D tray that looks like a New York taxi. The **Petrie Court Café** and, for a light bite, the **Roof Garden Café** (May–October) have nice views. Since 1925, the **Lexington Candy Shop** (1226 Lexington Ave., tel. 212/288–0057) has been serving milkshakes and malteds, cheeseburgers and crinkle fries to the luncheonette crowd. It's worth a trip back in time.

 5th Ave. and 82nd St.

212/535-7710;
www.metmuseum.org

 Suggested donation
$12 ages 12 and up,
$7 students

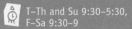 T–Th and Su 9:30–5:30,
F–Sa 9:30–9

 4 and up

Dendur, a real Egyptian temple moved here to save it from destruction. It's one of the most looked-at works of art in the museum.

On weekends and holiday Mondays, visitors are welcomed by special family greeters, easily spotted in bright red aprons in the Great Hall. Ask for self-conducting activity guides and recommended art-related programs offered free of charge for children and accompanying adults. Weekend programs for various ages are offered throughout the year and include Hello Met, Art Evenings for Families, Start with Art at the Met, Look Again, and the Charles H. Tally lecture series for families.

Prior to visiting, log onto the MuseumKids page of the museum's Web site for fun facts and a list of daily family programs, all free with admission. Go to Things to Do When Visiting and For Kids to Try Right Now! as well as the Explore & Learn section to plan your excursion or do interactive art activities.

HEY, KIDS! Did you know that the colored buttons given to visitors show that they have made a donation (for admission) to the museum? More than 100 colors are used, and 17,000 buttons of the same color are given out each day. Most are recycled.

KEEP IN MIND Strollers are permitted except on Sunday unless otherwise noted, but you can borrow back carriers for free at the 81st Street entrance. Those who are truly ambitious can visit the Cloisters at Fort Tryon Park as well as the Met, as your admission donation covers both on the same day. The Met's first-floor gift shop and second-floor Children's Shop stock unusual kids' toys, games, and books—good for birthday gifts that children won't already have. The MetKids catalog also offers items designed to help children learn and grow, many based on works in the museum's collection.

MUSEUM OF MODERN ART

Nicknamed MoMA, this museum was the world's first dedicated to the education and enjoyment of modern art. Today it maintains the world's foremost collection of 20th-century art: more than 135,000 paintings, sculptures, drawings, prints, photographs, architectural models and drawings, and design objects. In November 2004 the museum reopened its Midtown site, celebrating both its 75th anniversary and the completion of the most extensive renovation project in its history. The new museum has nearly double the capacity of the former building, encompassing approximately 630,000 square feet of new and renovated space.

From the lobby, you can enjoy stunning views of the Abby Aldrich Rockefeller Sculpture Garden (considered by some the museum's most distinctive feature) and its modern sculpture, seasonal plantings, and reflecting pools. Also from the lobby, you can take the staircase to the second floor, where you can find contemporary galleries, the museum's first gallery space specially designed for video and media, and galleries for prints and

KEEP IN MIND For a schedule of film and media programs and to determine if they are appropriate for children, call the museum or check the Web site. Family programs and gallery talks change periodically. Call Family Programs (tel. 212/708–9805) for information on activities and events for kids.

EATS FOR KIDS The **Modern,** a fine-dining restaurant on the first floor, may not be your first choice with kids, but two new tasty and tasteful cafés, **Cafe 2** (on the second floor) and **Terrace 5** (on the fifth), just might be. For scrumptious desserts, salad bar, sandwiches, and antipasto eat at **Mangia** (50 W. 57th St., tel. 212/582–5882).

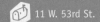 11 W. 53rd St.

 212/708-9400;
www.moma.org

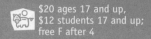 $20 ages 17 and up,
$12 students 17 and up;
free F after 4

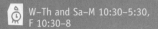 W–Th and Sa–M 10:30–5:30,
F 10:30–8

 4 and up

illustrated books. The third floor has galleries for architecture, design, drawings, photography, and temporary exhibitions. Fourth- and fifth-floor galleries contain paintings and sculptures. Each of these galleries is devoted to one subject, period, artist, or set of artists. The expansive skylit spaces of the sixth floor have 18-foot ceilings and more temporary exhibits. The lower level is home to the two refurbished Roy and Niuta Titus Theaters.

Innovative and creative family programs and gallery talks are offered throughout the year. A Closer Look for Kids ($5 per family), for children 5–10 with an adult companion, are themed talks about artwork in either the permanent collection or temporary exhibits. Tours for Fours is a popular preschool offering. Art Mix, for children 11–14, is another gallery talk series. Preregistration is required for some family offerings, while others are run on a drop-in basis. Be sure to call ahead.

HEY, KIDS! Before or after your visit, explore Destination Modern Art on the MoMA Web site. It's an animated intergalactic journey disguised as a cartoon and activity center just for kids. Don't forget to turn on the volume for the narration, and don't worry if you don't have Flash 6 (required to view the site). You can download it by clicking on the link. Learning about art was never this much fun.

MUSEUM OF TELEVISION AND RADIO

It's not hard to imagine what the attraction of this museum is, for students of radio and TV and families alike. The broadcast collection comprises more than 120,000 TV and radio programs and advertisements from the 1920s to the present, which your family can enjoy on any of the museum's individual consoles. Catch classic Jack Benny or early Ed Sullivan shows; watch the first moon walk, Uncle Milty, *I Love Lucy* reruns, or the Beatles' first appearance on American television. If you'd like to watch this vintage footage, get to the museum early. Go to the library, and search a computer database for the programs you want to view. Then view your selections in the Console Center. Many consoles can accommodate more than one viewer, so you can watch with other family members.

The museum also has three galleries exhibiting art and artifacts relating to television and radio as well as theaters for the museum's screening series. And since there's always something

EATS FOR KIDS For a meal on a bun, visit **Burger Heaven** (20 E. 49th St., tel. 212/755–2166; 536 Madison Ave., tel. 212/753–4214). For lunch, brunch, tea, or dinner, girls will delight in the **American Girl Café** (609 5th Ave., at 49th St., tel. 877/AGPLACE), on the third floor of this female-oriented retail establishment. The prix-fixe three-course menu is reasonable for adults, a little pricey for kids, but don't forget to try the warm cinnamon buns. Also see Radio City Music Hall and Rockefeller Center and the Ice Rink.

 25 W. 52nd St.,
between 5th and 6th Aves.

$10 ages 14 and up,
$5 children 13 and under

 T–W and F–Su 12–6, Th 12–8

212/621–6600;
www.mtr.org

4 and up, TV festival 4–10

new going on, regular visitors return frequently to check out the latest special screenings and temporary exhibits. Examples of recent exhibits include Miffy and Her Friends and the works of Jim Henson. A recent screening series included the whimsical clay animation of Nick Park, in Nick Park's World: The Eccentric Adventures of Wallace and Gromit.

A radio studio is also among the museum's facilities. Frequently throughout the year, live broadcasts, which are open to the public, take place here. Morning drive time, music, talk shows, and book chats are just some of the formats heard during these programs. By dropping in, families can see what happens behind the scenes of a radio show.

KEEP IN MIND
Visiting the West Coast? Drop by the Museum of Television and Radio in Los Angeles (465 N. Beverly Rd., Beverly Hills, tel. 301/786–1025). Become a member at either site, and you can visit both museums for free.

HEY, KIDS! If you're 9–13 and want to be on the radio, come for a Re-creating Radio workshop. No, you won't be the guest DJ on your favorite radio station—nothing that glamorous! Instead you can try re-creating performances and sound effects from shows of the '30s and '40s. Tickets ($7) must be purchased in advance by phone (tel. 212/621–6600) or in person at the museum.

MUSEUM OF THE CITY OF NEW YORK

Where in the world can you find seats from the original Yankee Stadium, a 1980 Checker cab, a piece of the old mechanical Times Square news "zipper," and a giant bolt tightener used to build the Brooklyn Bridge? At the Museum of the City of New York, of course! Chronicling 400 years of life in one of the world's greatest urban centers, the museum showcases Gotham's past, present, and future in permanent collections and special exhibitions. More than 1.5 million items include more than 2,000 paintings depicting the changing cityscape and 500,000 photographs documenting city history.

Since the four-story museum is too big to see in one visit, grab a floor plan and take a vote on what to visit. Though the Period Room Alcoves, representing domestic life from the late 17th to the early 20th centuries, may not be kids' favorite, the theater collection, including 3,500 costumes, might leave them starstruck. In the Fire Gallery, children learn about bucket brigades and see a hose carriage and pumpers that were pulled not by horses but by firefighters. The museum's collection of marine-related artifacts includes

EATS FOR KIDS They'll make 'em the way you like 'em at **Peter's Burger Place** (1413 Madison Ave., tel. 212/722–4400). If you'd rather make your own salad or get soup or a sandwich, head for **Shin's** (1414 Madison Ave., tel. 212/831–1754), a deli take-out joint with tables in a large room in back.

HEY, KIDS! Calling all kids! On Saturday from 12 to 1:30, bring your family for MCNY Kids gallery visits led by teen museum educators. Arts and crafts, fun, games, and special events are free with museum admission. Reservations aren't necessary, but a parent or caregiver must stay with you during this program. What are you waiting for? Be an MCNY kid!

 1220 5th Ave., at 103rd St.

 212/534–1672;
www.mcny.org

Suggested donation
$12 families, $7 adults,
$4 students 6–college

W–Su 10–5; T groups only

4 and up

ship models, ships' figureheads, and paintings. Youngsters are often fascinated by New York Toy Stories, which features a collection of 10,000 playthings from Colonial times to the present, including antique dolls, children's games, and an unusual collection of furnished dollhouses from 1769 to the 1970s.

Ongoing exhibitions highlight the museum's collections and embrace the past, present, and future of New York City. Protect! reveals how fire and fire safety have shaped the Big Apple over four centuries. Trade! looks at the changing role of the Port of New York City and how it factors into the city's economy. Perform! is a look at the always-changing comedies, dramas, and musicals of the Broadway stage.

If you want to find out how NYC got the nicknames the Big Apple and Gotham or the origin of the term "23 skiddoo," just ask the museum's research department. And while we're asking questions…Who *is* Major Deegan?

KEEP IN MIND To get an in-depth look at the exhibits before you go, check out the Web site's Museum Collections Sampler, which includes pictures and information. In addition, some items and exhibits can only be seen on the Web, including New York Footnotes, a collection of 18th-century women's shoes from the costume collection. Also check out the 19th-century New York City valentine. Updated daily, the site contains a calendar of family events, too.

NATIONAL MUSEUM OF THE AMERICAN INDIAN

Adults find both the interior and exterior architecture of this museum as interesting as its changing exhibitions of Native American artifacts. Children tend to be intrigued by the elaborate feathers, weavings and blankets, baskets, painted hides, Native American garments, and carvings. But whatever your family's interests, you can find plenty to see and do at this first museum of its kind dedicated to Native American culture.

In 1903 New Yorker George Gustav Heye began gathering a collection of 1 million Indian artifacts from North, Central, and South America. Eventually, it became New York's Museum of the American Indian, with Heye as director, but by late in the century it came under the Smithsonian umbrella, with the stipulation that it remain in New York. The National Museum of the American Indian also includes a research and conservation facility in Suitland, Maryland, and a museum on the National Mall in Washington, D.C.

KEEP IN MIND The museum offers programs of interest for the entire family that are fascinating, fun, and free, including the Native Sounds Downtown concert series. In May don't miss the weekend afternoon Children's Festival. Throughout the year the museum hosts plays, storytelling, dance, museum talks, and hands-on learning activities that share the ways and world views of native peoples. Screenings of documentaries and films by Native American filmmakers on contemporary subjects are shown daily. Information regarding these and other activities can be found on the Web site.

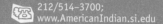 George Gustav Heye Center,
1 Bowling Green

212/514–3700;
www.AmericanIndian.si.edu

 Free

 F–W 10–5, Th 10–8

9 and up

One of the most visited museums in New York, the center occupies the first two floors of the Alexander Hamilton U.S. Custom House, a beautiful Beaux Arts–style building that is both a National Historic Landmark and a New York City Landmark. Outside are 44 columns, each adorned with the head of Mercury, the Roman god of commerce. Inside in the rotunda, a 140-ton skylit dome appears to soar overhead without any visible means of support. The symmetry of the Great Hall is complemented by monumental arches and columns.

Three main galleries feature exhibitions from the museum's renowned permanent collection and significant traveling exhibits from other institutions. Religious and cultural items are on display only with the approval of the appropriate tribes. A resource center on the main floor contains a wide array of materials on Native American history and culture.

EATS FOR KIDS
Ruben's Empanadas (15 Bridge St., tel. 212/509–3825) offers no-frills but unbelievable empanadas, favorably reviewed by critics, parents, and kids alike. At **Bubby's** (120 Hudson St., tel. 212/219–0666), go for a sandwich, fish, or breakfast 'til late afternoon.

HEY, KIDS! Outside the building's huge entrance are four large sculptures representing America, Asia, Europe, and Africa. The America statue features a Native American figure peering out from behind a throne. He wears a feather headdress and is surrounded by a totem pole and broken southwestern pottery. In 1907, when this customhouse was built, that Indian figure was meant to symbolize the vanishing Native American.

NBC STUDIOS TOUR

I t's not a sure bet that you'll see any television stars, but you never know whom you may bump into on NBC's studio tour. But that shouldn't be the main reason to take this hour-plus behind-the-scenes tour. The real reason is to learn fascinating secrets of television production.

NBC has been offering tours since 1933. An NBC page serves as your guide through the peacock network, and who knows? Your page may go on to become famous, like former pages Ted Koppel, Willard Scott, Regis Philbin, Steve Allen, Kate Jackson, and Michael Eisner.

Along your journey, you'll go back in time to NBC's birth in the Golden Age of Radio. Then you'll fast-forward to the days before fast-forward buttons, through landmark TV programs that your parents may have watched. Walk your way to the present through current studios, which might include those for two or three of the following: *Saturday Night Live, NBC Nightly News, Late Night with Conan O'Brien, The Jane Pauley Show, Deborah*

EATS FOR KIDS At the **Rock Center Café** (20 W. 50th St., tel. 212/ 332–7620), ask for a seat overlooking the skating rink in winter, the garden in spring–summer. Fans like **Mickey Mantle's** (42 Central Park S, tel. 212/688–7777) for its large portions, friendly service, oversize TV screens, and sports memorabilia.

HEY, KIDS! Before or after your tour, stop for a treat at the NBC Sweet Shop (right next to the tour desk!). Check out the 3-D floor map of New York City. As you walk "among" the famous landmarks, you can peruse and pick from an endless supply of colorful, eye-catching candy. Then munch your goodies on old-fashioned park benches overlooking Rockefeller Plaza.

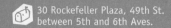 30 Rockefeller Plaza, 49th St. between 5th and 6th Aves.

212/664-3700, tapings 212/664-3056 or 212/664-3057; www.nbc.com/store

 $17.75 ages 17 and up, $15.25 children 6–16

 M–Sa 8:30–5:30, Su 9:30–4:30; hrs extended in summer

6 and up

Norville Tonight, and *Dateline NBC.* You can also learn about the latest TV technology used to broadcast around the world. Representatives from Kodak will take your photo on the set of the Tour Studio, where one lucky guest will report the weather. Because of fast-breaking events and changes in broadcast schedules, this unstaged tour varies from day to day.

The tour includes a small NBC museum that's part of a retail attraction called the NBC Experience, directly across from *Today*'s Studio 1A, on the corner of 49th Street and Rockefeller Plaza. The museum features memorabilia from NBC's long history—items like the first Howdy Doody test pattern, a microphone from early radio, a bottle from the original *I Dream of Jeannie,* and tons of photos. Here also you can explore some free interactive attractions with your favorite NBC personalities, like Al Roker and Bob Costas, on tape. Souvenir photos of you and your coanchors are available for a fee.

KEEP IN MIND There are a few things to remember about buying tickets. A discount ($15.25 per ticket) can be had for groups of as few as four people. Individual tickets can be purchased in advance by phone or on-line with a credit card, and you can also buy a combination ticket that includes a tour of Rockefeller Center (tel. 212/664–7174). Because so many groups book ahead of time, if you do choose to purchase your tickets on the day of your tour, you'll want to get here early. Tours are often sold out by early afternoon.

NEW VICTORY THEATER

Surprising as it sounds, this is Manhattan's first theater especially for families and kids. Its year-round season of professional productions by national and international artists is offered at surprisingly affordable prices. Reopened in 1995 as part of the theater district redevelopment, New York's oldest active theater was built in 1900 by Oscar Hammerstein. In 1902 impresario David Belasco took over the theater. Dramatic and vaudeville shows continued until 1932, when Billy Minsky opened Broadway's first burlesque in this theater. Next it was renamed the Victory, in the patriotic spirit of WWII, and ran second-run films for several decades. In the 1970s it became the block's first XXX-rated movie house. It seems emblematic of the whole Times Square face-lift that from these cultural ashes arose a phoenix for families.

Along the way, it became "reel" famous, too, making appearances in such movies as *Manhattan Murder Mystery*, the original *Shaft*, *Taxi Driver*, and, most recently, *The Siege*. Renovation began in 1994, restoring the striking facade with its monumental second-floor entry

KEEP IN MIND The "New Vic" is wheelchair accessible, but wheelchair seats must be purchased in advance. In addition, some performances are sign-language interpreted. Booster seats for small children are also available. The benefits of membership include 30% discounts on tickets, priority seating (tickets available to members before they go on sale to the general public), a member-friendly exchange policy, newsletters, various contests, and coupons for local restaurants and other establishments. Both members and the general public are invited to free pre-performance workshops conducted by theater professionals. Each workshop highlights an activity related to the day's performance, such as juggling or dance.

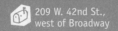 209 W. 42nd St.,
west of Broadway

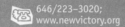 646/223-3020;
www.newvictory.org

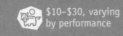 $10–$30, varying
by performance

 Times vary

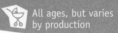 All ages, but varies
by production

staircase and globed standing lights. Inside, the opulent domed auditorium looks almost as it did as the Belasco Theater. Around the rim of the regal central dome are eight plump pairs of golden cherubs, whose feet dangle over the seats below. During the theater's renovation, the angels needed only one little repair—fixing a big toe. Adding to the elegant interior are tiers of box seats capped by golden domes. The two-balcony auditorium now holds 500 seats.

Cutting-edge family entertainment features masters of music, dance, drama, puppetry, and circus arts. Recent performances have included the *Circus Oz, Cookin',* *A Year with Frog and Toad,* and *Dance Cuba.* Performance times vary from just under an hour to two hours, and shows usually run two to six weeks. VicTeens, a program for kids 13–18, lets them see a show in a teens-only section of the theater and gives them food, free stuff, and a chance to hang out with the show's cast. How cool is that?

EATS FOR KIDS
Try lunch, brunch, or dinner at **Zuni** (598 9th Ave., tel. 212/765-7626) for reasonable prices and southwestern flavors with Asian and Italian flair. You can't go wrong at **John's Pizza** (260 W. 44th St., tel. 212/391-7560). Also see restaurants in Broadway on a Budget.

HEY, KIDS! Now here's something to buzz about: If you count all the bees in the theater's wall moldings (added by David Belasco in 1902) and all the bees on the seat fabric (added by the New 42nd Street Inc. in 1995) plus all the ones on the metal chair sides at the end of each row, just how many bees are there in the New Victory? Final answer: There are 31,566 bees. Un-bee-lievable!

NEW YORK AQUARIUM

"By the sea, by the sea, by the beautiful sea . . ." That little ditty conjures up images of crowded old seaside attractions like Coney Island. Alongside the cotton candy and amusements, however, is this aquarium, which first welcomed visitors in 1896 at its former site in Manhattan's Battery Park and moved to this 14-acre location in 1957. It's home to more than 10,000 species of marine life, including beluga whales, giant sea turtles, sand-tiger sharks, and sea otters.

Don't miss the sea lion demonstrations in the 1,600-seat Aquatheater, but don't sit too close either, unless you're prepared to get splashed. Get touchy-feely with a horseshoe crab in the touch tank (May–October). Marvel at the re-creation of a rocky Pacific coast habitat for the aquarium's black-footed penguins, gray and fur seals, sea otters, and Pacific walruses. Watch them from below water inside or from above water around rocks, trees, and pools outside. Try to attend one of the feedings throughout the day.

EATS FOR KIDS Eat a packed lunch on the Oceanic Deck or near Explore the Shore, or buy from the outdoor **snack bar** or indoor **Seaside Cafe.** Try boisterous, Italian **Gargiulo's** (2911 W. 15th St., tel. 718/266–4891) or **Totonno Pizzeria Napolitano** (1524 Neptune Ave., tel. 718/372–8606). The boardwalk has fast food.

HEY, KIDS! Take a "get wet" workshop, and prepare for oceans of fun. You can share the magic and mystery of the marine world through art, music, science, beach walks, lectures, tours, and other adventures. Free public events also are scheduled, ranging from an Amazon Adventure to the Halloween Sea Monsters program. Or dive right in and spend the summer as a Marine Explorer or Junior Oceanographer.

 Boardwalk at W. 8th St.,
Coney Island, Brooklyn

 718/265–FISH;
www.NYAquarium.com

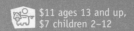 $11 ages 13 and up,
$7 children 2–12

 Daily 10–5

 All ages

In Explore the Shore, your family can stand under a 400-gallon tidal wave that crashes every 30 seconds. A Plexiglas hood keeps you dry, but the power of the sea may leave you breathless. Hands-on exhibits, interactive videos, games, and marine tanks teach about the ecology of the oceans and marshlands. Check out the cool state-of-the-art wave machines.

Come within inches of 9-foot sharks patrolling their 90,000-gallon tank. At the aquarium's newest exhibit, Alien Stingers, you can come face to face with mysterious sea jellies. By the end of your visit, you might just be humming the rest of that ditty: "We'll have fun, we'll have fun, oh how happy we'll be!"

KEEP IN MIND A family membership in the Wildlife Conservation Society costs only $100 and lets everyone in your family visit the aquarium and the Bronx, Central Park, Prospect Park, and Queens zoos free for a year. Quite the bargain! You also get a year's subscription to *Wildlife Conservation Magazine*, a great read and valuable supply of school report pictures and articles for kids from kindergarten to college. (Trust me: You'll want to save these issues.)

NEW YORK BOTANICAL GARDEN

This 250-acre National Historic Landmark has 48 gardens and plant collections including outstanding orchids, daylilies, flowering trees, and conifers; wetlands; ponds; a cascading waterfall; a 5-acre tract of the original forest that once covered the city; and dramatic rock outcroppings. But the reason families visit is the Everett Children's Adventure Garden, the first indoor/outdoor museum of botany and horticulture built especially for children. Its hands-on activities, imaginative exhibits, and fanciful gardens are exciting and inviting.

Stop at the visitor center for a free map and to check activity schedules. Then head for the Boulder Maze; explore its winding trail, and climb up to look through the discovery scope at the wetlands below. Next enter Beth's Maze, and find your way around the hedges. Sit or step on the oversize lily pads of the Sun, Dirt, and Water Gallery, and watch water shoot up. A giant frog topiary leaping from a splashing fountain invites you to discover how plants make food, move water, and use sunlight.

KEEP IN MIND The botanical garden is less crowded on weekdays, except Wednesday, when admission is free. A narrated tram tour, which runs every 30 minutes, lets you explore various places and spaces and reboard. On a hot day, it's the only way to travel, and remember the folding umbrella stroller. Guided walking tours on Wednesday, Thursday, Saturday, and Sunday as well as Monday holidays are probably best suited for older children. Bird walks in spring and fall are also free, as are audio tours of the conservatory's World of Plants, the Ross Conifer Arboretum, and the garden grounds, also available in a children's version.

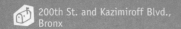

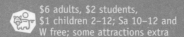
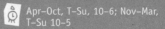

In the Wonder Gallery, kids can invent a plant or wander through vine-covered tunnels, tiny bridges, and a minipond. At the outdoor Pond Gallery, kids can pretend to be a pond-dwelling animal. They can take a water sample and see what's in it, make a giant bird's nest, or visit the Plant Touch Tank. The Enid A. Haupt Conservatory, the nation's largest Victorian glasshouse, showcases rain forest plants, desert galleries, and numerous palm trees under glass.

The Children's Adventure Garden is part of the Children's Adventure Project, which also includes the Mitsubishi Wild Wetland Trail and the Ruth Rea Howell Family Garden. Along the wetland trail, children can get a close-up view of this fascinating ecosystem and discover What Stinks, an interactive exhibit about how wetlands recycle plants. In the family garden, visitors can dig; investigate ponds, insects, and plants; and meet gardeners from around the world. During the winter holidays, the Holiday Train Show in the conservatory adds to the fun.

HEY, KIDS! Among the amazing plants here are the Venus's-flytraps. A bug a day keeps the plant doctor away. At 200 feet, the Kapok tree is one of the rain forest's tallest trees. Feeling hungry? Look for the cacao plant. Chocolate comes from seeds in its reddish brown pods.

EATS FOR KIDS The indoor/outdoor **Garden Cafe** and the **Vistor Center Cafe** serve kid-oriented comfort foods. Picnic tables are located at the Clay Family Picnic Pavilions, outside the Everett Children's Adventure Garden. Outside the garden in the Belmont section, also called Arthur Avenue, try one of the many pizza parlors and Italian restaurants. **Dominick's** (2335 Arthur Ave., tel. 718/733–2807) has inexpensive family-style Italian fare.

NEW YORK CITY FIRE MUSEUM

I n a renovated three-story firehouse built in 1904, you and your family can view one of the most comprehensive collections of fire-related art and artifacts from the 18th century to the present. Large firehouse doors, the housewatch (front desk) entrance, stone floor, brass sliding pole, and hose tower remind visitors of the former home of Engine Company 30, its firefighters, its rigs, and its horses. The nonprofit museum operates in partnership with the New York City Fire Department, which owns the building and provides the collection and the firefighters who serve as tour guides.

Permanent and temporary exhibitions chronicle the evolution of fire-fighting technology beginning with the early bucket brigades. Carefully preserved hand-operated, horse-drawn, and motorized equipment; toys; models; fire engine lamps (running lights from horse-drawn equipment); presentation silver; oil paintings, prints, and photographs; "fire marks" (emblems on buildings denoting the brand of insurance carried); and folk art illuminate the traditions and lore of fire fighting.

EATS FOR KIDS Hankering for Cajun cooking and cowgirl memorabilia? Head to the **Cowgirl Hall of Fame** (519 Hudson St., tel. 212/633–1133). **Brothers Bar-B-Q** (225 Varick St., tel. 212/727–2775), a bi-level barnlike space, serves chicken and ribs; on Monday night, it's all-you-can-eat.

KEEP IN MIND As tempting as it is to children, please remind them that there's no climbing in this museum. The building can get crowded when group tours visit, so call ahead to see if schools are scheduled when you're planning to come. The museum also hosts birthday parties for children 4–8, and you can get fire-themed goodies from the museum store. To preview some of the museum's exhibits, read more about museum history, or get updates on family programs, visit the museum Web site.

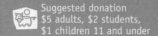 Suggested donation
$5 adults, $2 students,
$1 children 11 and under

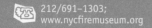 278 Spring St.

212/691–1303;
www.nycfiremuseum.org

T–Sa 10–5, Su 10–4

 2–11

Organized fire fighting began in New York City in 1648, when eight fire wardens, nicknamed the Prowlers, patrolled the streets from dusk to dawn. These patrols were also called the Rattle Watch, as wooden rattles were the first fire alarms. Before phones were introduced in 1882, fire companies used the telegraph and a system of Morse code and bells to communicate fire emergencies across the city.

Preschoolers and early schoolers can learn why fires were a big problem in olden days and how bucket brigades worked. They may be fascinated by how men pulled and pumped the early fire engines and how horses and dogs helped. They may also discover how fire fighting changed as New York grew from a small village to a large city. Older students may be interested in the evolution of fire alarms, in the duties of today's firefighters, and in the teamwork involved in fighting fires. A Fire Safety exhibit especially for families features hands-on activities and information for whatever type of house or apartment you live in.

HEY, KIDS! Create your own scavenger hunt. On the first floor, look for those wooden rattles used as the first fire alarms. Since dogs have always been firehouse mascots, search for a dog collar. Can you locate an early motorized fire truck that was started with a hand crank? On the second floor, find the fire chief's sleigh and the engine with an eagle on top. This pumper rode in the parade for the newly unveiled Statue of Liberty more than 100 years ago.

NEW YORK CITY OPERA YOUNG PEOPLE'S WORKSHOPS

No need to sing the praises of opera when you can experience it with your family at Lincoln Center. New York's amazing performing arts center is filled with theaters of all shapes and sizes, playing host to every type of music imaginable, dance, film, and even the circus. Of these, opera (the center is home to both the Metropolitan and New York City operas) is perhaps the least accessible for many children, but not to worry. The New York City Opera Young People's Workshops, offered by the New York City Opera education department, provide an energetic and exciting kid-oriented introduction to this musical and theatrical art form.

These one-hour interactive workshops are designed especially for families. Prior to select weekend matinee performances, City Opera staff and artists conduct hands-on activities that explore the themes, drama, and music of the afternoon's opera. Everyone is encouraged to join in the fun, which may include acting out a scene, learning a dance, examining costume design, or exploring a musical score. Four family-friendly operas are usually chosen

HEY, KIDS! If your interest has been piqued by the magic of opera, ask a parent if you can take a backstage tour of the Metropolitan Opera House (30 Lincoln Center Plaza, tel. 212/769–7020), October–June. Marvel at castle construction in the carpentry shop, suits of armor and Cinderella gowns in the costume shop, and big hair and bald pates at the wig-maker's shop. Peek into the rehearsal room, auditorium, dressing rooms, and cafeteria. Tours ($9 adults, $4 children 4–12), recommended for those 8 and up, are weekday afternoons and Saturday mornings. Reservations are advised for this 1½–hour tour, and potty stops are not included.

New York State Theater, Lincoln Center,
62nd St. and Columbus Ave.

 $5

 Sa–Su 12–1

212/870–5643;
www.nycopera.com

 6–12

each season. Sessions have included such operas as *The Magic Flute, The Mikado, Porgy and Bess,* and *Carmen.* Advance reservations (which can be made online at the City Opera Web site) are required for the workshops, held at the New York State Theater between noon and 1. Doors, at the stage entrance, open at 11:30, and curtain is at 1:30.

If you need to brush up on your Verdi, Mozart, or Puccini, visit the New York City Opera Web site and access the Learning and Resource Centers. You can read biographies, explore an opera glossary, and locate plot descriptions so you can read the story before or after you hear the opera. And if you're wondering what to wear, pretty much anything goes these days. Some families do enjoy the occasion to dress up, but the key is comfort. Remember the aim is for everyone to have fun.

EATS FOR KIDS

Café Vienna (Avery Fisher Hall, tel. 212/874–4700) serves sandwiches for lunch on matinee days. Though the adult fare is fabulous at **SQC** (270 Columbus Ave., tel. 212/579–0100), the real treats are the organic baby food (tofu puree, anyone?) and the kids' menu (hot chocolate is a must). Even adults order from it.

KEEP IN MIND Like its bubbling, dancing fountain, Lincoln Center is overflowing with wonderful family performances, from jazz to the circus, ballet to movies. Here's just a handful: the Chamber Music Society's Meet the Music Concerts for Kids (tel. 212/875–5788), Movies for Kids (tel. 212/875–5600), and the New York City Philharmonic's Young People's Concerts (tel. 212/875–5656).

NEW YORK CITY POLICE MUSEUM

Four blocks south of the South Street Seaport, in the first police precinct station (1911) in downtown Manhattan, the New York City Police Museum gives an inside look at the dedicated men and women who serve and protect the city that never sleeps. Three floors of exhibits depict a rich history that dates back to Colonial times, when "watchmen" patrolled the cobblestone streets of New Amsterdam.

Begin at the oak front desk on the first floor, used from 1931 to 1999 at the Bronx's 46th precinct. Tour the Transportation Room to find both easily identifiable and unusual methods of police transportation, from bicycle patrols to the 1972 Plymouth Fury used in such movies as *The French Connection, Coogan's Bluff,* and *The Seven-Ups.* The Communications Room and the Look of the Law are also on this level.

The Transit and Housing police departments are saluted on the second floor. Here, too, you'll find the most photographed museum exhibit: the jail cell. Notorious Criminals

EATS FOR KIDS
In addition to serving adult fare, **Les Halles** (15 John St., tel. 212/285–8585), a French bistro with butcher paper on the tables, accommodates young diners with macaroni, french fries, and the like. Also see restaurants listed for the South Street Seaport, Fraunces Tavern Museum, and Federal Hall National Memorial.

KEEP IN MIND
The Hall of Heroes is the museum's most solemn room, containing the shields of every NYPD officer killed in the line of duty since the department began in 1845. In the Firearms Training Simulator (FATS), visitors 18 and older are allowed to hold a real firearm. Gripping photographs, news footage, and interviews with NYPD first-responders are part of 9.11 Remembered, a moving tribute to the courage and sacrifice of the men and women of the NYPD. These exhibits may not be suitable for your children. Parental discretion is advised when visiting these three areas of this extraordinary museum.

 100 Old Slip
(between Water and South Sts.)

 212/480-3100;
www.nycpolicemuseum.org

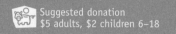 Suggested donation
$5 adults, $2 children 6–18

 T–Sa 10–5

 8 and up

and Weapons of the Trade includes mug shots and gangster weapons, such as Al Capone's machine gun. Most remember him from Chicago, but he actually got his notorious start in the Big Apple. The third floor contains the Wall of Valor, the Hall of Heroes, the Firearms Training Simulator, and special exhibits.

Your child's most memorable moments here may include playing detective in the Interactive Crime Scene, which re-creates a crime in a city apartment. Follow the actual steps investigators use to solve crimes, from collecting evidence to questioning witnesses. Continue the game of cops and robbers as your child poses for pictures dressed in a police uniform or takes part in a make-believe lineup, all while learning about the brave men and women who keep our communities safe.

HEY, KIDS! Did you know that the word "cop" was first used in 1845, when police shields were made of copper? Speaking of metal and medals, the first police department Medal of Valor was designed by the famous jeweler Louis Tiffany, the son of the founder of Tiffany & Co. Its design, with a superimposed N and Y (the logo of the New York Yankees) remains the same today.

NEW YORK HALL OF SCIENCE

New York City's only hands-on science and technology museum is also one of the country's best. With more than 250 interactive exhibits over 35,000 indoor square feet (not to mention 30,000 outdoor square feet in the Science Playground), the hall is, scientifically speaking, *the* place to bring the family for a day of fun and learning.

The ground-level main hall contains Seeing the Light and Sound Sensations: The Inside Story of Audio, where kids jump and dance while their shadows "play" music. They can also compose a jazz melody and electronically change their voices.

The lower level contains Hidden Kingdoms of the World of Microbes, with the largest collection of the world's smallest creatures; the Realm of the Atom; and Marvelous Molecules—The Secret of Life, about the shared chemistry of all organisms. In the Biochem Lab, the world's first hands-on lab that's open to the public and devoted to the chemistry of living things, you can conduct your own experiments with step-by-step instructions and help from staff.

KEEP IN MIND Students with A's in both math and science can receive a free one-year Honors Membership to the museum, just another reason to hit the books. As for history, the hall of science is in Flushing Meadows–Corona Park, site of the 1939 and 1964 world's fairs. Also in the park is the Queens Museum of Art (tel. 718/592–9700), in front of which is the Unisphere, easily spotted from miles around. First displayed at the 1964 World's Fair, this massive sculpture of the earth is 140 feet high and made from 380 tons of stainless steel.

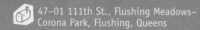 47–01 111th St., Flushing Meadows–
Corona Park, Flushing, Queens

 718/699-0005;
www.nyhallsci.org

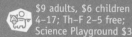 $9 adults, $6 children
4–17; Th–F 2–5 free;
Science Playground $3

July–Aug, M 9:30–2, T–F 9:30–5,
Sa–Su 10:30–6; Sept–June, M–Th
9:30–2, F 9:30–5, Sa–Su 12–5

 2 and up, Science
Playground 6 and up

The upper level's Great Hall is home to traveling exhibits and the permanent Living Carpet, a large-scale interactive floor installation that lets you explore and influence the emotional landscape of the carpet. Don't miss the floor ballet of six interacting human silhouettes. Nearby is the kid-pleasing bubble area, where you and yours can create life-size bubbles or raise a bubble wall. From the Great Hall you can exit outside to the Science Playground.

A 300-seat auditorium serves as a showcase for videos, films, lectures, and special events. Demonstrations are scheduled daily throughout the facility. In the Preschool Science Place, little hands can investigate sound, color and light, simple machines, and measurement in a self-contained space apart from the bustling crowds. A 55,000-square-foot expansion in 2004 includes terrific exhibits: the redesigned Rocket Park; the Search for Life Beyond; and Connections—The Nature of Networks.

HEY, KIDS! Don't miss the Science Playground (March–December), the Western Hemisphere's largest outdoor laboratory of exciting whole-body experiences. Compose a tune with your feet on Sound Steps. Talk softly into the red Whisper Dish, and marvel when a friend across the playground can hear you.

EATS FOR KIDS There are no restaurants really close by, so plan to pack a lunch and find a spot in the spacious 300-seat **dining hall** overlooking the park and Science Playground. No time to make a bag lunch? You can purchase sandwiches, snacks, and beverages from vending machines once you get here. The dining hall is available for children's birthday parties.

NEW-YORK HISTORICAL SOCIETY

Founded in 1804, the New-York Historical Society is New York's oldest museum, predating the founding of the Metropolitan Museum of Art and the American Museum of Natural History by nearly 70 years. Today it serves as a collective memory of the heritage of New York City, the state, and our nation, exploring the connections between past events and our present-day lives. More than 1.6 million items can be found here, among them the nation's largest collection of Tiffany glasswork and 433 of the 435 original watercolors from John J. Audubon's *Birds of America* (1827–38). Also included in the museum collections are American folk art paintings, toys, weathervanes, George Washington's camp bed from Valley Forge and his inaugural armchair, the desk at which Clement Clark Moore wrote "A Visit From St. Nicholas" in 1822, and a chair made for Marie Antoinette's private chambers at Versailles. In all, it's home to one of the country's greatest collections of American art and historical artifacts.

EATS FOR KIDS For some of the city's tastiest bagels, go to **H&H Bagels** (2239 Broadway, at 80th St., tel. 212/595–8003). **EJ's Luncheonette** (447 Amsterdam Ave., between 81st and 82nd Sts., tel. 212/873–3444) is a sure bet for heaping portions of kid comfort food. Try the black-and-white malt. **Sarabeth's** (423 Amsterdam Ave., between 80th and 81st Sts., tel. 212/496–6280) is a crowd pleaser, especially for brunch. Don't miss the French toast, red omelet, and delectable pumpkin muffins.

 170 Central Park West, between 76th and 77th Sts.

 212/873-3400; www.nyhistory.org

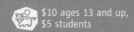 $10 ages 13 and up, $5 students

 T–Su 10–6

9 and up

In the Great Hall exhibits such as Presidential Treasures (from the library collection), which highlights manuscripts from American presidents, are installed on a rotating basis. The Henry Luce Center displays objects from the museum's collection. Visit the Web site to take a virtual tour of past exhibits; your kids might like Petropolis: A Social History of Urban Animal Companions, which treated the place of pets in our history.

The society holds regularly scheduled reading and craft programs for children and families that complement current exhibitions. Live performances in the arts, film festivals, walking tours, museum programs, and lectures round out the wide variety of events offered to families throughout the year.

KEEP IN MIND
During the school break between Christmas and New Year's, the society celebrates the holiday season with special morning family programs. Call the main phone number for a detailed schedule and registration information.

HEY, KIDS! Be on the lookout for Inspector Collector, a.k.a. Harley Spiller, who has been known to host fabulous and fun family workshops on collecting. The inspector shows how collecting everyday items like spoons, postcards, and even chewing gum can teach us about American history and culture.

NEW YORK LIBERTY BASKETBALL

It's fast-paced, it's fun, it's family entertainment, and it's affordable. If this doesn't sound like today's professional sports to you, you haven't been to a New York Liberty game. The area's hot WNBA (Women's National Basketball Association) team brings summer basketball to Madison Square Garden crowds of just less than 20,000, averaging second in overall attendance in the WNBA. It's not uncommon to spot celebrities like Rosie O'Donnell, Julia Stiles, Knicks legend Patrick Ewing, Spike Lee, or rocker Joan Jett in the crowd. The New York Liberty was also the first professional sports team to play at Radio City Music Hall (while Madison Square Garden was used for the 2004 Republican National Convention).

Each season has 32 games, with half played at home at the Garden. Games usually run under two hours, unless overtime is called. Arrive early—gates open one hour before game time—to watch the pregame shoot-around and team warm-up. Technically, no photographs are permitted, but young fans with cameras do snap shots of their favorite players before the games. Don't forget to get your souvenir team yearbooks.

EATS FOR KIDS
A popular chain known for its family cuisine, **T.G.I. Friday's** (484 8th Ave., tel. 212/630–0307) has good burgers, sandwiches, and salads. **Seven** (350 7th Ave., between 29th and 30th Sts., tel. 212/967–1919) serves up tasty soups and overstuffed sandwiches. Also see eateries listed for Madison Square Garden.

HEY, KIDS!
And hey, basketball fans and surfers! Log on to the Liberty's Web site to catch up with your favorite team. You can e-mail questions to the head athletic trainer or directly to the team, send fan mail to the players, play fun games, test your Liberty knowledge, or print coloring pages of the players. Other features take you behind the scenes to learn all about the team and the game. You can also click to find out about special promotions and giveaway nights. And if that's not enough, New York Liberty runs a girls' summer basketball camp (tel. 212/924–4040 Ext. 106) each year. It's a slam dunk!

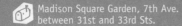 Madison Square Garden, 7th Ave. between 31st and 33rd Sts.

212/564–WNBA; www.nyliberty.com

 $8 and up

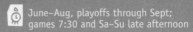 June–Aug, playoffs through Sept; games 7:30 and Sa–Su late afternoon

 5 and up

During the games look for Maddie the Mascot, a friendly overgrown dog who makes friends with the fans, leads the conga lines on the court, and leads the cheers. Named for Madison Square Garden, Maddie often signs autographs and poses for pictures in the lobby before the games. Also part of the excitement here is the 12-member dance-and-performance team, Torch Patrol. This athletic, high-energy squad of young men and women conduct fun, frenzied mayhem during time-outs, incorporating tumbling, dance, and crowd interaction. At each game, the arena's most spirited section of fans is chosen to attend a postgame autograph session with team players, so get your wave ready and make your cheer loud and clear. And don't even think about leaving your seat during halftime, or you'll miss the entertainment. When was the last time you got to see Frisbee-catching dogs or bike stunts? Don't try this at home. But do practice your hook shot and keep dribbling.

KEEP IN MIND Promotions take place during nearly every game. Whether it's miniball or sports-poster giveaways, mascot day, or fan appreciation T-shirt night, these special events give your kids another thrill just by walking through the turnstile and getting a free souvenir. The team also holds celebrations like Flag Day, Father's Day, and charitable game promotions like a Cheering for Children Auction and Breast Cancer Awareness Night. If you have a choice, pick a game where they're giving something away.

When is a museum not an ordinary museum? When it's housed in a decommissioned 1936 subway station in downtown Brooklyn. The New York Transit Museum is a walk-up, sit-down, and touch museum that is home to 100 years of transit history and memorabilia. The collections include 19 restored subway cars dating from 1904 to 1964, as well as antique turnstiles, a working signal tower, a surface transportation room, and a variety of other transit equipment.

Revolving exhibits, programs, workshops, and tours provide an insider's look at MTA bridges, tunnels, subways, buses, and commuter railroads. You and your children can watch a film clip about the age of Els (elevated trains) before they fade into history. Take the A Train or catch all the trains you missed in an exhibit of full-size classic wooden cars and their modern counterparts. Or see a sign of the times in a display of nearly 200 examples of subway signage: in porcelain enamel, cast iron, brass, wood, and plastic. Pass through the first automated turnstiles. Drive a city bus, or better yet, don't miss the museum's annual Bus Festival, in

EATS FOR KIDS The **Armando Ristorante** (143 Montague St., tel. 718/624–7167) offers traditional Italian fare at more than fair prices. For lunch or dinner, hit the **Heights Café** (84 Montague St., at Hicks St., tel. 718/625–5555). Parents find much to choose from on the eclectic American/international menu, and kids can't go wrong with a standard burger or pizza. For other food choices, see the Brooklyn Academy of Music and Brooklyn Botanic Garden.

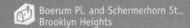 Boerum Pl. and Schermerhorn St.,
Brooklyn Heights

 $3 adults, $1.50 children
3–17; some workshops charge

 T–F 10–4, Sa–Su 12–5

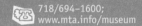 718/694–1600;
www.mta.info/museum

 2 and up

late spring or early summer. An entire block is shut to park historic buses outside, including a wooden open-top double-decker bus and a favorite, the 1949 Jackie Gleason bus, modeled after the one driven by Ralph Kramden on *The Honeymooners*.

In 2004 the launch of the Transit Museum's education Web site, Education Station, coincided with the commemoration of the 100th anniversary of the NYC subway. An interactive portal called Community Crossing features the Subway Centennial Student Activity Depot, with student-centered educational activities.

Shopping for a (subway) token of your affection to give to a (nostalgic) loved one? Look no further than the Transit Museum Gallery and Store. For transit-related toys, trinkets, and memorabilia, this is the place. In addition to the shop inside the museum, there's another one at Grand Central Station, adjacent to the Station Masters' Office. Admission to the Museum Gallery at Grand Central is free.

HEY, KIDS! Each year the museum conducts some nifty workshops just for kids. You can build a working model of a suspension bridge, make your own bus model, or create poetry in motion by writing your own poster poem like the ones on subways and buses.

KEEP IN MIND The museum offers guided tours of different parts of the transit system—in Manhattan, the Bronx, Queens, Brooklyn, Staten Island, and Long Island. Some include excursions to historical and cultural destinations. Because some tours involve strenuous walking and stair climbing, wear sturdy and comfortable shoes and clothes. Bring your MetroCard or tokens for travel, but first call ahead for reservation information and fees.

NY WATERWAY FERRIES

18

In the early 1800s, New Yorkers traveled to and from Manhattan by ferry, but as bridges and tunnels were constructed, ferries fell out of favor. Today you can experience this form of transportation on NY Waterway, the largest private ferry operation in the nation. NY Waterway transports more than 7 million passengers into the city each year on 22 vessels covering eight ferry routes. For commuters, ferries offer a shortcut to Manhattan minus the traffic jams, tunnel and bridge tolls, and parking problems usually associated with car travel. Ferry crossings run anywhere from five to eight minutes, with frequent departures throughout the day.

Ferries aren't just for commuters, however. If your family wants to sightsee, you can take a fun-filled ride and glide to ports of call in and around New York—to the beach at Sandy Hook, New Jersey; around lower Manhattan; and up the Hudson River, just to name a few. Most terminals offer all-day parking, and a free private shuttle bus system operates throughout the city, providing service to tourists, commuters, and downtown residents.

HEY, KIDS!

If you're taking a ferry to a Yankee game, why not make it a double-header of sorts? Ask your parents to find out about tours of Yankee Stadium (see #1). Highlights include the dugout, press box, clubhouse, and Monument Park.

KEEP IN MIND The best sightseeing bargain in the city is the free 20- to 30-minute ride on the Staten Island Ferry (tel. 718/390–5253) across New York Harbor. Take the older model blue-and-orange ferries, which sail higher in the water and have outside deck space, so you can enjoy views of the Manhattan skyline, the Statue of Liberty, Ellis Island, the New Jersey shore, and the Verrazano Narrows Bridge. Ferries run every 30 minutes during the day and evening and every hour after midnight and on weekend mornings.

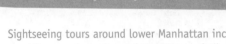
Terminals in Manhattan and New Jersey

800/533–3779;
www.nywaterway.com

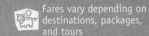
Fares vary depending on destinations, packages, and tours

Schedules vary, depending on route

2 and up

Sightseeing tours around lower Manhattan include harbor cruises by day and twilight cruises providing up-close views of the Statue of Liberty, Ellis Island, and the Brooklyn Bridge. You can also take a ferry to see the Mets or Yankees play ball. Packages include ferry transportation, a ticket to the game, a hot dog and beverage, and a souvenir. Dining and Broadway show packages are also available.

Hudson River cruises include tours of the legendary Rockefeller family estate in Pocantico Hills and historic Philipsburg Manor, a working Dutch Colonial farm; a Sleepy Hollow Cruise, including Sunnyside, the home of Washington Irving, and Philipsburg Manor; a scenic trip down the North Hudson River without stops; and a cruise to Lyndhurst, a great Gothic revival–style estate. But as nice as these sights are, what's really special about the tours is seeing New York from the water.

EATS FOR KIDS Some boats have a **snack bar** selling snacks, soft drinks, and cocktails. On some sightseeing cruises, box lunches are served, and passengers often take them ashore and eat at the historic sight being visited. Dining packages include reservations at various city restaurants. If you're taking NY Waterway from Weehawken, New Jersey's Port Imperial Terminal, consider eating right at the marina at **Arthur's Landing** (Pershing Rd., Weehawken, NJ, tel. 201/867–0777), which has a kids' menu.

PROSPECT PARK

Prospect Park offers 526 acres of winding paths, rolling hills, open spaces, Brooklyn's only forest, and other great green places to stroll, picnic, fly a kite, or sit and think. Designed by the renowned team of Olmsted and Vaux, it's home to the 90-acre Long Meadow, one of the city's greatest open spaces, with spectacular views of grass, trees, and sky. Feed the ducks and spot the swans at 60-acre Prospect Lake (Brooklyn's only freshwater lake), or stroll through the Oriental Pavilion.

If you want to ice-skate, head for the Wollman Rink from mid-November to early March, near the Lincoln Road entrance. It's the only open-air rink in the borough. Skate rental and instruction are offered. Most of the rest of the year, this is the place to rent pedal boats, which seat four—a great way to take a break and a tour of the lake at the same time. Tennis anyone? Visit the tennis center, open year-round at the Parade Ground (tel. 718/436–2500).

EATS FOR KIDS **Circles Restaurant** (192 Prospect Park W, tel. 718/499–5595) is next to the historic Pavilion Theater, once a single-screen movie house but now a multiplex. It can accommodate any size group. **Kate's Corner Snack Bar** (Wollman Rink) is open Thursday–Sunday. The **Songbird Café** (Audubon Center) is a natural place for a nosh. At **Second Helpings** (448 9th St., tel. 718/965–1925), an organic eatery and juice bar, kids can sample chicken, mac & cheese, PB&J, or grilled cheese, while adults indulge in sumptuous wraps on flat bread with homemade cumin chips. Yum! Also see the Prospect Park Zoo.

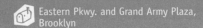

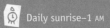
A 1912 carousel, in operation from April to October but not every day, features 51 magnificently carved wooden horses, along with a lion, giraffe, deer, and dragon-drawn chariots. This magnificent piece of Americana, originally installed at Coney Island, is at the Willink entrance at the intersection of Empire Boulevard and Flatbush Avenue. For live animals, head to the Prospect Park Zoo (*see* #16).

The Lefferts Historic House is one of Brooklyn's few surviving 18th-century Dutch Colonial farmhouses. Take a short walk to the nation's first urban Audubon center, at the Boathouse. A great place of discovery, it has hands-on exhibits and runs family programs with crafts and music Thursday–Sunday. The restored Beaux Arts–style Boathouse houses the electric boat *Independence,* which takes spring and summer tours of the park's waterways. Also here are aquatic discovery cruises, bird-watching tours, and twilight cruises.

KEEP IN MIND
Prospect Park hosts special community events, including Hawk Weekend in September, New Year's Eve fireworks, Earth Day Weekend in April, You Gotta Have Park in May, Macy's annual Fishing Contest, and the Celebrate Brooklyn! Arts Festival. It's no surprise more than 6 million locals and tourists visit each year.

HEY, KIDS! For a haunting good time, join the Halloween Haunted Walk and Festival, held throughout Prospect Park the last Saturday in October from noon until 3. (A carnival, with performances, games, and treats, takes place near the Nethermead, the geographic center of the park.) You'll be in ghoulish company as thousands of visitors walk along the haunted park pathways. Watch out for witches, ghosts, goblins, and other creatures that go bump in the night—or, in this case, the afternoon.

PROSPECT PARK ZOO

This 12-acre zoo, completely revamped and transformed into a modern children's wildlife learning lab, is home to 82 species of animals. Naturalistic habitat exhibits have replaced bars, cages, and pits, and the larger species that were part of the original menagerie of the late 1800s and early 1900s are gone.

Enter the Animal Lifestyles building, and your children will find air, water, and land animals in exhibits related to the center's wildlife education program. Reptiles, amphibians, fish, birds, and small mammals help highlight the environments they live in and their adaptations to their homes. The centerpiece of the building is the 4,500-square-foot hamadryas baboon exhibit. Perched high on the rock cliffs by an impressive waterfall, separated from these fascinating social primates by an invisible sheet of glass, their somewhat less fascinating primate cousins (humans) feel very much a part of this exhibit. Don't be surprised if a friendly baboon approaches the glass to study you back.

GETTING THERE You'll find entrances off Flatbush Avenue and near the Lefferts Historic House. If you drive, you can find free parking on Flatbush Avenue. By public transportation, take the subway's S or Q train to the Prospect Park station or the B41, B47, or B48 bus.

HEY, KIDS! Want to really experience animal habitats? Visit the World of Animals' 2½-acre Discovery Trail. Burrow in Plexiglas-topped tunnels, and pop up next to a prairie dog. Leap-frog across lily pads to goose nests, and pretend to hatch. In the Wallaby Walkabout, you can walk among these small Australian kangaroos and other animals, and in the 2,500-foot aviary at trail's end, you can walk around free-flying African birds and climb into nests your size. Willoughby Wallaby Whew!

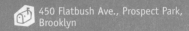
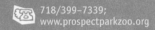
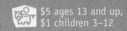
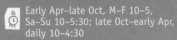

Drawing supplies are provided in the Animals in Our Lives building. Playful meerkats, emerald tree boas, saw-whet owls, and poison dart frogs call this space home. In the barnyard, kids can peek into the chicken coop or meet goats, sheep, and cows. California sea lions frolic in a rocky California coast–like environment. They are fed daily at 11:30, 2, and 4; it's a special treat (for them and you).

Interactive educational—often musical—shows at the Wildlife Theater (Memorial Day–Labor Day, Thursday–Monday) are good for the whole family. On weekends at 11 and 3, Keeper Chats highlight a different animal each month, as a zookeeper shares animal facts and fun with the audience. The zoo also sponsors special community events—the Fleece Festival, Keeping up with Keepers, Boo at the Zoo, and Make a Wish for Wildlife—free with admission. All in all, it makes for wonderful family fun.

EATS FOR KIDS A **cafeteria** is near the sea lion pool. Visit the **Second Street Café** (189 7th Ave., tel. 718/369–6928) for lunch or brunch. Order soup and some raisin-studded bread pudding. Try **Two Boots** (514 2nd St., tel. 718/499–3253) for creative pizzas (including Cajun and pizza-face personalized pies), Mac and Cheese Louise, or, for adventurous kids, pasta jambalaya. (Can you guess why it's called Two Boots?) **Tom's Restaurant** (782 Washington Ave., tel. 718/636–9738) is a family business with a friendly waitstaff and hearty diner fare.

PUPPETWORKS

For more than 35 years, the Puppetworks, Inc., under the artistic direction of Nicolas Coppola, has been known throughout the country for its mostly marionette productions. In 1987 Puppetworks opened a permanent 75-seat theater in a Park Slope (Brooklyn) storefront, next to the Puppetworks workshop. This informal and family-friendly theater presents daily performances of children's literature classics, with weekdays reserved for groups (20 or more). Puppetworks also hosts private showings of their programs for on-site birthday parties on weekends from 3:45 to 6:15. You supply the cake; they supply the entertainment and the clean-up.

Classic puppet theater favorites like *Puss in Boots, Rumpelstiltskin,* and *Pinocchio* may round out a year-round season that might also include the *Wizard of Oz,* a gala *Carnival of the Animals, The Frog Prince, Peter and the Wolf,* and *The Emperor's Nightingale.* Each production is faithful to its source, whether it's children's literature or international or national fairy or folk tales.

KEEP IN MIND Since 1976, when Macy's built a gingerbread puppet theater for Puppetworks, more than 50,000 children and their families have attended the annual Puppetworks Christmas performances. Bring your family to the ninth floor of Macy's Herald Square (Broadway at 34th St., tel. 212/695–4400) and start a new tradition. The holiday-themed performances are given 10 times daily and cost only a few dollars. In 1999 Macy's built a new puppet theater for these always festive and well-attended family puppet programs.

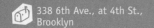 338 6th Ave., at 4th St., Brooklyn

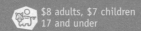 718/965-3391; www.puppetworks.org

 $8 adults, $7 children 17 and under

 Sa–Su 12:30 and 2:30

3–12

Just two puppeteers are responsible for each performance, and while each show averages 13 puppet characters, some have had up to 68 puppets. Professionally designed sets with distinctive painted backdrops and intricate puppet costumes give the feeling of a slightly scaled-down Broadway show. At the end of many performances, a professional puppeteer will bring out one of the beautiful, hand-carved puppets to show to the audience, giving a brief behind-the-scenes—or, more accurately, above-the-strings—talk about the workings of a puppet theater. Children are encouraged to ask questions. If your kids are truly enchanted by the experience, you can purchase a whimsical hand or string puppet on the Web site. Though not made by Puppetworks, these puppets are quite appealing—budget-wise too. Prices range from $20 to $30.

EATS FOR KIDS
For comfort food and diner delights (fluffy Belgian waffles, bacon-wrapped meat loaf, and stick-to-your ribs BBQ ribs), visit **Dizzy's** (511 9th St., tel. 718/499-1966). Also check out the restaurants in the Prospect Park Zoo and Prospect Park listings, including **Two Boots**.

HEY, KIDS! The walls of the Brooklyn Puppetworks theater display close to 100 marionettes used in past performances, though many are reused and recostumed. Can you identify the characters or the stories they come from? If you can't, let your imagination wander. Try to think of fairy tales you know. Who's the scariest villain, the cutest animal, your favorite character? Do any of the puppets you see look like them, and how do they differ from the way you would have created them?

QUEENS COUNTY FARM MUSEUM

A farm in New York City? Just barely. At the very edge of Queens, the Queens County Farm Museum occupies New York City's largest remaining tract of natural, undisturbed farmland. The landmark farmhouse and the 7-acre farmyard that make up the museum are just a small piece of the 47-acre Adriance Farm Park.

The farm was started in 1772 and passed through a series of owners until 1927, when New York State purchased the farm for Creedmoor Psychiatric Hospital, to provide both fresh produce and therapy for its patients. Staff and patients raised crops and livestock until the program was discontinued in 1960. Through the Colonial Farmhouse Restoration Society of Bellerose, organized in 1975, the farm's historic structures were preserved and the site was turned into a city park.

Pick up a map and take a self-guided tour of the farm museum. Begin at the centerpiece of the restored farm: the colonial farmhouse, where much of the original 18th-century

HEY, KIDS!
Contribute to the Fund-A-Friend program, and you can get a certificate and your name will be included on a display at the farm. Funds raised are used for feed and veterinary care, from $8 for a chicken or duck to $100 annually for a "caretaker," helping all the animals.

KEEP IN MIND Of the many family programs here, most carry a fee and some require reservations. (A calendar of events is listed on the farm Web site.) Activities have included a fall Apple Festival; the Amazing Maize Maze, a 2-acre corn maze; fall pumpkin picking; the Barnyard Easter Egg Hunt; arts and crafts workshops in winter and spring; New York's Annual Antique Auto Show; the Queens County Fair; and the Thunderbird American Indian Mid-Summer Pow Wow. A summer program of arts, crafts, and nature courses for children 6–10, comprising three two-week sessions, is also offered.

 73-50 Little Neck Pkwy.,
Floral Park

 Free; some events charge

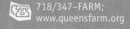 718/347-FARM;
www.queensfarm.org

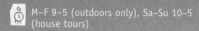 M–F 9–5 (outdoors only), Sa–Su 10–5
(house tours)

 1 and up

plank floors, beamed ceilings, wainscoting, paneling, doors, window glass, and hardware has survived. Other areas available for touring include the duck pond, the herb garden, and the orchard. A chicken coop houses 100 free-range hens producing 260–290 large brown eggs each laying cycle. The eggs are collected daily and washed and boxed for sale. Your children can visit Daisy, an Ayrshire cow, in the cow shed and stroll by the sheep pastures to survey the grazing livestock. Fields are planted with corn, pumpkins, tomatoes, and other vegetables as well as a 1-acre vineyard.

Each season the farm wears a new face, whether it's welcoming newborn barn animals in spring or picking the fresh produce of summer, stomping through the snow paths in winter or crunching a crispy autumn apple. The Queens County Farm Museum offers a thick slice of farm life to you and your family, painting a picture of the city's rich agricultural past.

EATS FOR KIDS You can't beat the price or the selection at the lunch buffet at **Pizza Hut** (253–11 Hillside Ave., Bellerose, tel. 718/343–1118). Thanks to kids' meals, you can feed a child for under $4 and yourself for under $7. Hop on over to **IHOP** (248–16 Northern Blvd., Little Neck, tel. 718/224–1178), short for the International House of Pancakes, to indulge in breakfast all day long. It's a surefire bet for pancake lovers, especially kids who love different flavored syrups.

QUEENS ZOO

Once upon a time, Flushing Meadow played host to the 1964 World's Fair. A zoo opened on the fairgrounds in 1968, and in 1992 it was completely revamped, transforming itself into this small but friendly 11-acre zoo, home to 400 animals of some 40 species. Here you can come face to face with a mountain lion, see South American spectacled bears at play, and watch Roosevelt elk roaming the range.

You can walk on the wild side from one coast of the United States to the other. Visit re-created habitats from a northeastern forest to the Great Plains to the rocky California coast. You won't want to miss sea lion feedings daily at 11:30, 2, and 4. Stroll from the forest floor to the treetops of the zoo's walk-through aviary (a geodesic dome designed by Buckminster Fuller for the World's Fair) to view a variety of birds. Check out the new exhibit of thick-billed parrots, an endangered species. Cross the covered viewing bridge of the coyote exhibit to peek into a window on their world.

EATS FOR KIDS Feed your animal appetite at the **cafeteria,** overlooking the sea lion pool. Visit **Uncle George's** (33–19 Broadway, Astoria, tel. 718/626–0593) for great cheap, hearty, home-style Greek cuisine, or try the **Omonia Café** (32–20 Broadway, Astoria, tel. 718/274–6650) for a light bite and people-watching.

53-51 111th St., Flushing Meadows–
Corona Park, Flushing, Queens

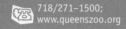
718/271-1500;
www.queenszoo.org

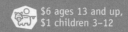
$6 ages 13 and up,
$1 children 3–12

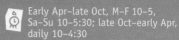
Early Apr–late Oct, M–F 10–5,
Sa–Su 10–5:30; late Oct–early Apr,
daily 10–4:30

All ages

The marsh exhibit forms a habitat for ducks, geese, herons, egrets, and turtles. The bison range lets you watch these fascinating American symbols from various points, giving the effect of the Great Plains of long ago. A waterfall, additional trees, and rock formations have improved the habitat for the endangered South American spectacled bears. Don't forget to say hi to Claire, the bald eagle named for former Queens Borough President Claire Shulman.

On the domestic side of the zoo, youngsters can meet and touch goats, sheep, and rabbits in an inviting planted space where they can also see a llama, Vietnamese pot-bellied pig, zebu, Jersey steer, donkeys, and such feathered friends as a Peking duck and Rhode Island Red. Despite its size, the zoo offers something for just about everyone.

HEY, KIDS! Shows at the Wildlife Theater include songs, audience participation, and educational programs for the animal-lover in you. They're given Memorial Day–Labor Day, Thursday–Monday, and times are posted on the domestic side of the zoo.

KEEP IN MIND The zoo is next to the New York Hall of Science, both in Flushing Meadow Corona Park. Combine your visit to either place with a stop at the nearby Queens Museum of Art (New York City Building, tel. 718/592–9700) to see the 9,335-square-foot scale model of New York City—complete with 895,000 tiny buildings and landmarks—originally made for the 1964 World's Fair.

RADIO CITY MUSIC HALL

You may have watched an awards show broadcast from Radio City Music Hall or even attended a performance here, but to get behind the scenes of this lavish art deco palace that's home to the high-kicking, smart-stepping Rockettes, you'll want to take the Stage Door Tour. The brainchild of theatrical impresario S. L. "Roxy" Rothafel, owner of New York's Roxy Theater, Radio City was the first building in the Rockefeller Center complex and the world's largest indoor theater in 1932. In 1999 it was renovated at a cost of $70 million. Tours showcase the building's technological capabilities as well as its history. Luminaries such as Frank Sinatra, Ella Fitzgerald, and Sammy Davis, Jr., have graced this stage, as have contemporary artists including Bette Midler, Sting, and 98 Degrees.

To whet your appetite, here are some amazing Radio City facts: Some of the curtains can create steam and rain, and the shimmering gold curtain is the largest theatrical curtain on earth. The mighty Wurlitzer organ, built in 1932, has two consoles, each weighing 2½ tons. Its pipes, some of which are 32 feet tall, are housed in 11 rooms. Look up

HEY, KIDS!
Imagine all the people and events that have graced this famous stage: from Madonna to Barney, the MTV Video Music Awards to the Tonys. The movies *Snow White and the Seven Dwarfs, 101 Dalmatians, Miracle on 34th Street, The Lion King,* and *GoldenEye* all premiered here.

KEEP IN MIND In 1979 to save the music hall from the wrecking ball, the program format was changed from films and stage shows to live concerts, television specials, and events. The *Radio City Christmas Spectacular, Sesame Street Live,* and adult as well as kid concerts play to sell-out crowds throughout the year. You must purchase a ticket for children 2 and older for performances here, but for some events, like Barney, youngsters 1 and older require a ticket, even if they plan to sit in your lap for most of the show.

 1260 6th Ave., at 50th St.

 Tours daily 11–3 every ½ hr

212/247–4777 tour, 212/307–7171
events; www.radiocity.com

Tour $17 ages 12 and up,
$10 children 11 and under

7 and up

and you can see a 24-carat gold-leaf ceiling glistening 60 feet above you. For the electrical record, the music hall contains over 25,000 light bulbs inside; outside, the marquee is a block long and has more than 6 miles of red and blue neon.

The Stage Door Tour also includes a visit to the private apartment of founder Roxy Rothafel and a stop in the costume shop, which contains examples of lustrous outfits worn by the Rockettes, the world's most famous precision dance troupe. Your tour group will also meet a member of the Rockettes, who will share some of the company's history. One-hour tours depart from the main lobby at the corner of 6th Avenue and 50th Street.

And once your family has taken the tour, consider joining the more than 300 million people who have seen movies, concerts, special events, and stage shows here over the years, and see all that technological wizardry at work yourselves.

EATS FOR KIDS Take your pick (or your children's pick) of local theme restaurants, each with eye-appealing memorabilia and kid fare. Music fans sing the praises of the **Hard Rock Cafe** (221 W. 57th St., tel. 212/459–9320). Movie buffs marvel at **Planet Hollywood** (1540 Broadway, tel. 212/333–7827). Board a spaceship to planet Mars for a crater burger, galactic cheese sandwich, or full moon pizza at **Mars 2112** (1633 Broadway, tel. 212/582–2112).

ROCKEFELLER CENTER AND THE ICE RINK

Skating at the Ice Rink at Rockefeller Plaza is enchanting, twinkling, festive, and fun, and it's spectacular when the huge Christmas tree casts its long shadow. (It arrives in mid-November, and the lighting ceremony is shortly after Thanksgiving.) It may not be the biggest rink in the world, but skating here certainly is one of the big New York experiences. Sessions are 1½ hours, and admission is on a first-come, first-served basis. Skate and locker rentals, season passes and multiticket books, lessons, and group rates are all available, as are birthday parties (January–April). Teens get a bit exuberant during evening skates and the pace is faster, but day or night, it's a skate to remember.

But the ice rink is just a small part of the 22-acre complex known as Rockefeller Center, one of the world's most famous pieces of real estate. There are actually 19 limestone and aluminum buildings here, and tours of the complex as well as combination tickets including a tour of NBC studios (see #29) are available. Or explore the center on your own, before or after your skating session.

KEEP IN MIND Other great spots for a twirl on the ice are the Lasker and Wollman Memorial rinks (see Central Park), the latter offering a magical experience beneath the city skyline; Sky Rink (see Chelsea Piers); the World's Fair Ice Skating Rink (New York City Building south wing, Flushing Meadows–Corona Park, Queens, tel. 718/271–1996); the Staten Island Skating Pavilion (30–80 Arthur Kill Rd., Staten Island, tel. 718/948–4800), for year-round fun; and Brooklyn's Wollman Rink (see Prospect Park), not to be confused with Central Park's similarly named facility. Contact each for prices, hours, and seasons.

Bordered by 47th and 52nd Sts. and 5th and 7th Aves.; ice rink, between 49th and 50th Sts. and 5th and 6th Aves.

212/332–7654 rink, 212/332–7655 lessons, 212/664–7174 tours

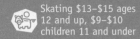
Skating $13–$15 ages 12 and up, $9–$10 children 11 and under

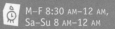
M–F 8:30 AM–12 AM, Sa–Su 8 AM–12 AM

2 and up

Travel this complex moving east to west, following a trail punctuated by three famous statues from Greek mythology. Atlas stands guard outside the International Building (5th Ave. between 50th and 51st Sts.). Head one block south on 5th Avenue and turn west to stroll along the Channel Gardens, which lead from 5th Avenue to a stair connected to the Lower Plaza. Six rock pools are surrounded by flower beds filled with seasonal plantings in a setting conceived by artists, floral designers, and sculptors who present 10 shows each year. Somehow it manages to look great in any season. Below on the Lower Plaza, locate the famous gold-leaf statue of Prometheus, towering heroically over the ledge. The entrance of the 70-story GE Building (30 Rockefeller Plaza), once known as the RCA Building but now referred to as "30 Rock," is also guarded by another striking statue of Prometheus. It all makes Rockefeller Center a landmark of epic proportions.

EATS FOR KIDS
Dine at the new **Rink Cafe and Bar,** open in summer 11–11, or the **Rock Center Café** (*see* NBC Studios Tour). **Dean & DeLuca** (1 Rockefeller Plaza, tel. 212/664–1363) serves quick sandwiches and snacks. See also the Museum of Television and Radio and Radio City Music Hall.

HEY, KIDS! The GE Building houses NBC headquarters (*see* NBC Studios Tour), and some of the first television programs originated from here. Nowadays *Today* broadcasts from a ground-floor glass-enclosed studio at 49th Street and Rockefeller Plaza. Be here between 7 and 9 AM to try to join the backdrop of faces behind the show's hosts. Bring a colorful sign saying hello to a loved one or proclaiming your hometown (if you're from out of town). You might get on TV.

RYE PLAYLAND

Go for the rides. Go for the fun. Go to sun, swim, play, or walk around, but go to Rye Playland.

This National Historic Landmark, opened in 1928 and featured in such films as *Big, Fatal Attraction,* and *Sweet and Lowdown,* still counts seven of its original rides among its more than 50 rides. But the park also features new vertical thrill rides, water rides, and a separate Kiddyland just for the toddler set.

The carousel, built in 1915, is still going strong, and the trademark 82-foot Dragon Coaster is one of the last remaining historic wooden coasters in North America. Don't miss the new Super Flight Flying Coaster and Twister—well, perhaps parents would just as soon miss these sensory experiences. Also at the park are arcade games, the usual midway games, a lake with boat rides, minigolf, a beach, a scenic boardwalk, and an Olympic-size pool, all on Long Island Sound.

GETTING THERE The park is less than a 45-minute drive from the city. Take I–95 (the New England Thruway), and get off at Exit 19. Follow the signs to Playland Parkway. Or call Westchester County Bee-line Buses (tel. 914/682–2020) for schedules.

KEEP IN MIND Remember to bring all the essentials: swimsuits, towels, beach toys, sunscreen, and water bottles—especially for your younger thrill seekers. Unlike the rest of this beautifully landscaped park, Kiddyland has no natural shade (or cool breezes). Bring blankets or lawn or beach chairs if you're staying for a concert. And of course, bring money. Parking costs $5 weekdays, $7 weekends, and to ride the rides you can purchase individual tickets or ticket books ($9–$21), providing a reduced rate. Look for discount coupons in local magazines and newspapers, and if you find one, don't leave it at home.

 Playland Pkwy., Rye Beach

Free; most attractions charge

 May–Sept, T–Su, hrs vary seasonally

914/813-7000;
www.ryeplayland.org

All ages

Start your day at the beach or pool, before the sun gets too hot, and lunch and munch on the boardwalk. By afternoon, it's off to the rides, along with a round of minigolf and a boat ride. Rides usually open at noon, and Tuesday through Friday (the park is closed Monday, except for summer holidays and special events) is less crowded than weekends. Watch for costumed characters and strolling musicians, and catch a puppet show at the Kiddyland puppet theater. Be warned that Kiddyland gets crowded by midday, so you'll want to visit early or at dinner time. Entertainment, including evening concerts, is featured daily mid-June through Labor Day at the Music Tower Theater. Parents and kids can bop to songs of the '70s, '80s, '90s, and today. Fireworks displays are held every Wednesday and Friday night in July and August.

Maintained by the Westchester County Parks Department, this old-fashioned amusement park is a beautiful setting dotted with art deco buildings straight out of the 1920s, meticulously groomed flower beds, and grassy, shady malls for strolling. It's a delight!

EATS FOR KIDS It's hard to imagine coming here without letting your children sip slushies or get sticky with cotton candy for a snack break. There are sit-down tables and fast food galore throughout Playland, including favorites from fast-food giants **Burger King, Nathan's Famous, Carvel,** and **Ranch 1.** You can also pack a lunch and use the picnic tables. The foot-long kosher hot dogs, ice cream, candy apples, and fried dough are hard to resist. Cruise the boardwalk for additional fast-food fare.

SCHOMBURG CENTER

The Schomburg Center for Research in Black Culture, one of the research libraries of the New York Public Library system, is considered one of the leading institutions of its kind in the world. Devoted to the preservation of materials on black life, it's the guardian of more than 5 million items, including more than 3.5 million manuscript items, 170,000 books, and 750,000 photographs. Collections of magazines, posters, art objects, films, videotapes, audio recordings, and memorabilia are also included.

Tours, exhibitions, forums, film screenings, and performing arts bring black history and culture to life for both young and old. Thanks to a 350-seat state-of-the-art auditorium, a 75-seat theater/auditorium, and a 30-seat screening room, the Schomburg Center sponsors about 60 programs each year, including poetry readings, plays, concerts, lectures, and panel discussions. Regular exhibitions are mounted in the gallery and exhibition hall. The Art and Artifacts collection holds more than 20,000 items in three areas: paintings and sculpture, works on paper, and textiles and artifacts. It's particularly strong in art produced

HEY, KIDS! Inlaid in the floor of the airy lobby of the Langston Hughes Auditorium is *Rivers,* an artistic work that's a tribute to Hughes (1902–67), writer of plays, stories, books, newspaper sketches, and, most notably, poems. If you haven't read anything by him, read his poem "A Dream Deferred." He penned many of his Jesse B. Semple or "Simple" columns about Harlem life in a brownstone at 20 East 127th Street, between Madison and 5th avenues.

515 Malcolm X Blvd.

Free

M–Sa 10–6, Su 1–5

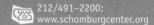
212/491–2200;
www.schomburgcenter.org

9 and up

during the Harlem Renaissance. Portraits of many famous 19th- and 20th-century black artists, politicians, actors, musicians, athletes, and social activists are included.

Visit Exhibition Hall to view Romare Bearden: From the Archive. Take time to look at Africana Age: African and African Diasporan Transformations in the 20th Century, an exhibit that details the political and cultural achievements and struggles of the black world during the last century. It also looks at the challenges facing peoples of African descent in this new century. Whether in sports, literature, politics, religion, music, entertainment, art, or other fields, people of African descent have made tremendous contributions to society despite unbelievable odds. See how many of these achievers you and your children recognize. Discuss the contributions each one has made to society. If your knowledge is lacking, there's no better place to learn about the influence of black Americans on our history and culture than the Schomburg Center.

EATS FOR KIDS Go to **Manna's Too!! Deli Restaurant** (486 Lenox Ave., tel. 212/234–4488) for breakfast, salad bar, fried chicken, and soul food buffets. For southern specialties, home-style cooking, and friendly service, try **Miss Maude's** (547 Lenox Ave., tel. 212/690–3100) or **Sylvia's** (328 Lenox Ave., tel. 212/996–0660).

KEEP IN MIND Other Harlem sights include the Abyssinian Baptist Church (132 Odell Clark Pl. W, tel. 212/862–7474), pulpit for two famous Adam Clayton Powells, one of whom was also a congressman. Tour the Apollo Theatre (253 W. 125th St., tel. 212/531–5337). The Studio Museum in Harlem (144 W. 125th St., tel. 212/864–4500), a small art museum, has a sculpture garden and a collection of paintings and photographs.

SONY WONDER TECHNOLOGY LAB

8

From the moment you're greeted outside the Sony Wonder Technology Lab by b.b. wonderbot, the interactive robot, you feel the excitement of cutting-edge communication technology. Enter your name, have your picture taken, and record your voice at the sign-in station, located at the twinkling fiber-optic lights, to obtain your personalized "swipe cards," which allow access to 38 interactive exhibits.

Don't be surprised if you see your picture or hear your voice pop up throughout your visit. You're not just going to see technology; you will become part of it during an adventure through four floors of hands-on educational fun. Don't despair if you and your kids are not techno-whizzes; helpful guides throughout the lab will answer your questions and offer assistance.

Okay. Roll 'em, as your children take part in a production in the television studio, perform with recording artists Bow Wow and Mark O'Connor, and experiment with sounds and

EATS FOR KIDS In Sony Plaza, a **kiosk** has bagels, sandwiches, and soups for a picnic in Central Park. **Mangia** (16 E. 48th St., tel. 212/754–7600) has sandwiches, salads, and antipasto. **Burger Heaven** (536 Madison Ave., tel. 212/753–4214) serves burgers, fries, and shakes.

KEEP IN MIND This place is a true bargain. Admission to this nifty wonderland of technology is free, as are screenings of popular movies shown evenings in the High Definition Theater. The lab also offers free and low-cost programs and events for parents and children throughout the year, including an annual Halloween celebration and screenings after school, on Thursday evenings, and during winter holidays. A schedule of family programs is on the Web site.

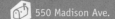 550 Madison Ave.

 212/833-8100;
www.sonywondertechlab.com

 Free

 T–W and F–Sa 10–6, Th 10–8,
Su 12–6

 All ages

images to create and view their very own movie trailer. They can visit the Environmental Command Center, where they'll need to gather and analyze data using the latest tools and technology in order to save New York City from an ecological disaster.

For a historical perspective, the Communications Bridge covers 150 years in the history and development of technology. Look for red circles along the way, which highlight important inventions. Just think . . . one day, all these exciting new technologies will just be red circles in some future historical display.

Finally, take a break in the 72-seat High Definition Theater, where you can sample the latest in High Definition Television, coming soon to a TV near you.

HEY, KIDS! He's a mess of wires, microchips, and a whole lot of at-titude. He's b.b. wonderbot, the lab's robot star and official greeter. Wonder how he can answer all the questions he's asked? Telepresence technology (a.k.a. remote control)! What's that? With miniature cameras hidden in b.b. wonderbot's eyeballs and microphones in his head, a human operator can see and hear people and direct the robot's remarkably lifelike movements and clever conversation.

SOUTH STREET SEAPORT MUSEUM

Nestled within a 12-block historic district of restored 18th- and 19th-century buildings and sailing ships, this museum actually comprises a number of facilities: a visitor center, Maritime Crafts Center, library, three floors of galleries in the landmark Schermerhorn Row, a fleet of sailing ships, and re-created printing shop. All are dedicated to chronicling the history of New York's original seaport and its commercial and cultural impact on the city, the state, and the nation.

Set sail for another place and time with a map and schedule from the visitor center. Whether it's a concert, a show by street performers, guided tours, or family programs, there's always something happening at the museum. Family Gallery Guides direct you around the world's largest collection of items related to New York's port. More than 2 million archaeological artifacts, fine and decorative folk arts, ship models, scrimshaw, and maps are showcased in the Schermerhorn Row galleries.

KEEP IN MIND Among the district's sights is the Titanic Memorial (Fulton and Water Sts.), a small lighthouse commemorating the 1912 sinking. Follow Fulton Street's cobblestones to Schermerhorn Row, a redbrick terrace of Georgian and Federal warehouses and counting houses, which showcases shops, restaurants, and the museum's galleries. Or take an early (3–8 AM) stroll through the Fulton Fish Market, the nation's largest and oldest (since the 1820s) wholesale fish market. During the warm months, the museum runs tours.

Pier 16 Visitors' Center,
12 Fulton St.

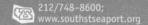
212/748-8600;
www.southstseaport.org

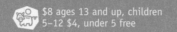
$8 ages 13 and up, children
5–12 $4, under 5 free

Daily 10–5

3 and up

Three historic museum vessels are open for tours, including the *Peking* and the *Wavertree* (large sailing cargo ships) and a lightship, the *Ambrose*. Explore the harbor on the *W.O. Decker,* a 1930 tugboat that worked this waterfront. Or climb aboard the *Pioneer,* a historic schooner, for a fun-filled sail. Sailing instruction for teens is offered on the *Lettie G. Howard,* a fully restored 1893 fishing schooner, now a National Historic Landmark.

Your family can visit the Maritime Crafts Center, where model-builders and a wood-carver ply their trades. At Bowne & Company Stationers, a re-creation of a 19th-century printing shop, artisans demonstrate the skills that made the city the nation's printing capital. On weekends, holidays, and school vacations, crafts workshops related to museum themes and exhibits are held. Performers and storytellers are also featured periodically.

HEY, KIDS! If a visit here tickled your sails, why not come back for more? Learn to furl a sail, tie a knot, or chart a course at one of the family programs scheduled every Saturday and Sunday throughout the year.

EATS FOR KIDS The Seaport is home to more than 35 restaurants and eateries from fast food to restaurant fare. Grab a burger, hot dog, pizza, or salad at the **Promenade Food Court** (Pier 17, 3rd floor). Don't miss the view from the tables in the glass-walled atrium. If deep dish is your wish, try **Pizzeria Uno Chicago** (89 South St., Pier 17, tel. 212/791–7999).

STATEN ISLAND CHILDREN'S MUSEUM

6

How would your children like to crawl through an ant home, watch a butterfly being born, or listen to an insect chorus? They can do that and more at the Staten Island Children's Museum. In an 82-acre park, the museum occupies 40,000 square feet of a four-story building with an Italianate facade and a renovated barn and connector building. An imposing porpoise, hanging in the central atrium, greets you. Exhibits tackle subjects from many different perspectives, incorporating the arts, science, and the humanities with an inviting child-friendly approach.

The Bugs and Other Insects exhibit invites big and not-so-big people into the miniature world of insects. If insects bug your kids, a quick trip to Block Harbor will put them back on an even keel. This waterfront setting, complete with pirate ship and gangplank, is an imaginative play space containing blocks and a menagerie of animal toys. In It's a Dog's Life, kids learn about animals' amazing abilities and body language as they see like a pigeon, hear like a cat, and smell like a dog. Daily storytelling and animal feedings are held here.

KEEP IN MIND Benefits of a family membership ($80) include advance notice of special events, sneak previews of new exhibits, members-only events, the museum calendar, and discounts on gift shop items, birthday parties, special programs, and summer mini-camps.

HEY, KIDS! There are so many different ways to "do" this museum. Want to watch the stars come out here? The museum sponsors sleep overs. Feel like celebrating? You can have a birthday party here, perhaps based on a museum exhibit, or a cooking, a chocolate, or an ice-cream party, too. Throughout the year, but especially during school holidays, the museum offers exciting programs and crafts workshops, free with admission.

 Snug Harbor Cultural Center,
1000 Richmond Terr., Staten Island

 $5 ages 1 and up

 July–Aug, T–Su 11–5; Sept–June,
T–F 12–5, Sa–Su 10–5

718/273-2060;
www.sichildrensmuseum.org

2 and up

Kids can jump on a fire truck, ring its bell, and slide down a firehouse pole in the Ladder 11 exhibit. Portia's Playhouse is an interactive theater space where kids try on masks or costumes and use props, puppets, sound effects, lights, and other theater equipment in imaginative play. The Walk-In! Workshop is a classroom activity center equipped with self-directed art activities and materials. In Great Explorations, three environments—tundra, rain forest, and ocean—let little tykes go on adventures, from driving a dogsled to diving deep to the ocean floor. Sea of Boats, an outdoor play space, includes a tugboat, lighthouse, dinghy, and other nautical knickknacks.

Founded in 1974 by a group of parents, the museum moved to its current site in 1986. Museum educators are always on hand to animate and explain exhibit themes and activities. School and community programs, traveling exhibits, family workshops, hands-on science activities, and performances of storytelling, dance, drama, and puppetry are all part of the fun and learning here.

EATS FOR KIDS **Ozōn,** a healthy-fare fast-food restaurant in the lower plaza here, serves fun food in a cool place. Try the baked sweet potato fries with marshmallow dip or the s'mores for dessert. You can get killer chili at **Adobe Blues Restaurant** (63 Lafayette St., tel. 718/720–2583), a southwestern-style eating place just off Richmond Terrace.

STATEN ISLAND ZOO

How many legs does an African millipede have? How far can a snowy owl turn its head? For the answers to these and other animal queries, visit the Staten Island Zoo. On 8 acres in a manicured park setting, New York City's biggest little zoo features an African savannah, aquarium, and tropical forest.

The African Savannah exhibit re-creates this ecosystem at twilight and features meerkats, a burrowing python, leopards, bush babies, and rock hyrax—curious creatures that look like rodents but are actually most closely related to elephants. The Tropical Forest exhibit highlights the endangered South American rain forest and the animals that dwell within. Here your family can watch the piranha, spider monkeys, short-tailed leaf-nosed fruit bats, and iguanas in a natural flow of flora and fauna.

The wraparound aquarium exhibit spotlights marine life from all over the world, whereas the Children's Center resembles a New England farm, complete with a covered bridge

KEEP IN MIND Plan your day at the zoo so you don't miss the action during feeding times. The reptiles chow down at 2:30 PM on Sunday. The sharks and piranha at the aquarium break for a bite at 1 on Thursday. (Don't worry. They do eat more than once a week; they just don't eat in front of an audience at other times.) Join the bats from 2 to 3 every day for a meal in the Tropical Forest.

 614 Broadway, Staten Island

 $5 ages 15–59, $3 children 3–14, W 2–4:45 donations accepted

Daily 10–4:45

718/442-3100; www.statenislandzoo.org

All ages

overlooking a duck pond. Here your children can meet an interesting array of international domestic farm animals. Be sure to visit the Pony Barn and Track for pony rides (additional fee).

Special programs are held throughout the year with some—like Maple Sugaring, Puppet Shows and Work Weather Gear—requiring preregistration and a nominal fee. Other events—like Leapin' Lizards, Fine Feathered Faces, Hats Off to Giraffes, Eat Like a Bird, and Children Against Litterbugs—are free.

The zoo is a great place to celebrate Groundhog Day. Chuck, New York City's only weather-predicting groundhog, greets visitors throughout the day after a 7:30 AM prediction proclamation. Hardy souls who brave the cold to cheer the resident rodent share coffee, juice, bagels, and the fun of witnessing Chuck's moment in the sun (or shadow).

HEY, KIDS! Snakes Alive! If you love things that slink and slither, check out the Carl Kaufeld Serpentarium, which features an internationally acclaimed display of reptiles. In fact, it has one of the most extensive collections of North American rattlesnakes anywhere.

EATS FOR KIDS Visit the **Zoo Café** (tel. 718/720–7218) for a convenient lunch or midday snack. Try **Duffy's** (650 Forest Ave., tel. 718/447–9276) for Staten Island's best burger and family dining. No reservations are taken, so expect a wait. **Nucci's Italian Restaurant** (616 Forest Ave., tel. 781/815–4882) is the place for pizza and Italian fare.

STATUE OF LIBERTY

4

"Give me your tired, your poor, / Your huddled masses yearning to breathe free. . . ." Many people recognize the opening lines of the poem "The New Colossus," which is inscribed on a plaque inside the Statue of Liberty museum. Everyone recognizes the sentiment. For more than 100 years, this historic monument has served as a universal beacon of hope and opportunity, a symbol of freedom, and a gift of international friendship. It's one of our nation's most heavily visited attractions, popular with both kids and adults. The official name of the statue is *Liberty Enlightening the World*.

The statue was sculpted by Frederic-Auguste Bartholdi, who first traveled to America in 1871 to propose the monument and choose a suitable site. Built in 1884 in France, the statue stood in Paris until it was dismantled and sent to the United States in 1885. A foundation and pedestal were created here, and the completed monument was dedicated on October 28, 1886. By the 1980s, a complete refurbishment was needed, and a team

EATS FOR KIDS There's a pleasant outdoor **café** on Liberty Island. You can also pack a picnic to eat along the way, or after your return on the ferry, go to one of the eateries mentioned in Ellis Island, Fraunces Tavern Museum, and South Street Seaport Museum.

KEEP IN MIND Security measures may affect your visit to this American treasure. For the latest information, visit the park's Web site. In summer, waiting in line can be hard on kids; bring water bottles, juice boxes, and small toys to amuse them. Saturday is more crowded than Sunday. The ticket office for both the Statue of Liberty and Ellis Island ferry service is at Castle Clinton National Monument (*see #57*). Free timed passes to enter the monument and enjoy its programs are available in limited quantities from the ferry company. You can reserve passes and ferry tickets in advance at 866/STATUE4 or www.statuereservations.com.

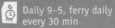

Liberty Island, New York Harbor

212/363-3200, 212/269-5755 ferry; www.nps.gov/stli, www.StatueofLibertyFerry.com

Free; Circle Line ferry, including Ellis Island and Statue of Liberty: $10 ages 13 and up, $4 children 4–12

Daily 9–5, ferry daily every 30 min

4 and up

of French and American artisans worked for two years repairing and replacing as necessary to keep the sculptor's original creation shining in the harbor. In 1986 the fruits of their labor were harvested, as the statue celebrated her centennial.

One of the main reasons to visit the statue, of course, is to view this monument to freedom up close. Due to increased security, visitors can no longer climb to the crown, but those who venture no farther than the pedestal will still have much to see and do. A museum here features exhibits detailing how the statue was built, and the promenade, colonnade, and top level of the pedestal offer spectacular views of New York Harbor. Life-size castings of the face and foot of the statue are available for sight-impaired visitors to feel. As she always has, Lady Liberty welcomes all.

HEY, KIDS! Since you can no longer go all the way to Lady Liberty's crown or torch, the next best thing is to get a good look at her through a ranger-guided tour. The promenade tour includes the museum in the pedestal's lobby, where the statue's original torch resides, as well as a visit to the promenade, which has great views of the statue and New York Harbor. The observatory tour covers much of the promenade tour plus an elevator ride to the pedestal observatory, with more awesome views, and a lighted view up into the copper interior of the statue.

THEODORE ROOSEVELT BIRTHPLACE

Though the building here isn't the real brownstone where Teddy Roosevelt was born—it's a 1923 reconstruction—it does teach a lot about the real life of the nation's 26th president. Five period rooms—the library, dining room, parlor (the most elegant room in the house), master bedroom, and nursery—are furnished with many items from the original house, pieces belonging to other family members, and other decorative period pieces. Two obelisks in the library are souvenirs of a family trip to Egypt. (Guided tours are given hourly.) In addition, two museum galleries display a variety of historical items, including journals, family photographs, articles of clothing including Roosevelt's Rough Rider uniform, and his crib.

The site offers a window on what mid-19th-century life was like for a wealthy family living on a once-quiet, tree-lined street in a most fashionable New York City neighborhood. Memorabilia reveals much about the man who would become not only president of the United States but also vice president, governor of New York, assistant secretary of the Navy, police commissioner, New York State assemblyman, and Rough Rider, as well as a rancher and cowboy.

HEY, KIDS! Do you have a favorite teddy bear? The teddy bear was actually named for Teddy Roosevelt, who once refused to shoot a captive bear on a hunting trip. Political cartoonists poked fun at the incident, but a Brooklyn toy maker asked Roosevelt's permission to make stuffed bears and call them "Teddy's bears." The upper museum room has one of these original bears along with cartoons, books, writing paper, ceramic figures, and other objects with teddy bear images. Does your bear look like one of "Teddy's bears"?

 28 E. 20th St.

 212/260-1616; www.nps.gov/thrb

 $3 ages 17 and up

 T–Sa 9–5

7 and up

As a young child, Theodore, called Teedie by his family, was a thin and sickly child who suffered from severe asthma. His father made the bedroom behind his nursery into an open-air porch by taking out a wall and putting up a railing. He also installed gym equipment so Teedie could exercise and improve his health. Roosevelt and friends used to climb through the nursery windows to get to the outdoor porch and equipment. He obviously overcame his frailty.

The Life and Times of Theodore Roosevelt, a 30-minute documentary narrated by Walter Cronkite, highlights Roosevelt's life, including scenes of 19th-century New York. *Teedie,* also a 30-minute film, tells the story of the young Teddy. Other biographical films are sometimes shown, and concerts, lectures, and special events are scheduled throughout the year.

KEEP IN MIND
Those interested in following TR through his later years should visit the Sagamore Hill National Historic Site (Cove Neck Rd., Oyster Bay, tel. 516/ 922-4788), on Long Island. Roosevelt's home for most of his adult life, it contains original furnishings and memorabilia.

EATS FOR KIDS For a spot of tea, some scones, and a light snack, visit **T Salon & Emporium** (11 E. 20th St., tel. 212/358–0506). For an endless menu, substantial portions, and reasonable prices, try **America** (9 E. 18th St., tel. 212/ 505–2110). Kids get crayons and coloring books, and a magician and balloon artist perform on weekends.

UNITED NATIONS

If you come on a working day, you'll see all 191 U.N. members' flags flying above 1st Avenue—from Afghanistan to Zimbabwe. It's an impressive sight, but so are the rest of U.N. Headquarters and the United Nations itself. Created in 1945, it joins countries working for world peace and against poverty and injustice.

As you enter headquarters gates, you're stepping into an "international zone," belonging not just to the United States but to all member nations. It has its own fire and security forces and its own postal administration, where you can post only mail bearing U.N. stamps. Mail a postcard to yourself as a souvenir, or stop by the bookstore for a memento.

One-hour guided tours include an explanation of the aims, structure, and activities of the organization as well as descriptions of art and architecture featured en route. Tours are given in many languages. What else would you expect at an institution with six official languages: Arabic, Chinese, English, French, Russian, and Spanish?

EATS FOR KIDS The **coffee shop** (public concourse) is open daily—first-come, first-served. The **Comfort Diner** (214 E. 45th St., tel. 212/867-4555) serves big portions of home-style food.

HEY, KIDS! You've heard of the Magic School Bus? Now you can ride on the CyberSchool bus (www.un.org/pubs/cyberschoolbus). This Web page offers a wealth of information, activities, and resources about the United Nations and worldwide concerns. Plan to "take a ride" before or after your visit. There are online puzzles and games for all ages. Try the Flag Tag or the Water Quiz. Check out live on-demand Webcasts 24/7, or click on InfoNation, an interactive database that lets you compare information about several countries at a time. (Great for schoolwork!)

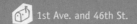 1st Ave. and 46th St.

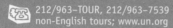 212/963-TOUR, 212/963-7539
non-English tours; www.un.org

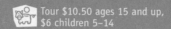 Tour $10.50 ages 15 and up,
$6 children 5–14

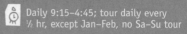 Daily 9:15–4:45; tour daily every
½ hr, except Jan–Feb, no Sa–Su tour

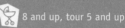 8 and up, tour 5 and up

On most days, tours take in many of these areas: General Assembly, Security Council Chamber, Trustee Council Chamber, Economic and Social Council Chamber, Rose Garden, lobby, and public concourse. In the lobby, noteworthy gifts to the U.N. include a model of Sputnik I from the Soviet Union, moon rock from the United States, a statue of Poseidon from Greece, and a 15-foot by 30-foot stained-glass Chagall window presented by the artist in memory of Secretary General Dag Hammarskjold. Other artworks include the mosaic *Dove of Peace,* presented by Pope John Paul II, in the General Assembly lobby; *Non-violence,* a bronze replica of a revolver tied in a knot, from Luxembourg, outside by the General Assembly building; and a Norman Rockwell mosaic, near the Economic and Social Council Chamber, inscribed, "Do unto others as you would have them do unto you." In truth your children might practice the golden rule better than some U.N. members, but amazingly, after over 50 years, this organization still strives to unite very disparate nations.

KEEP IN MIND Surfing isn't just for kids. At the U.N. home page, you can take an online tour before your visit; get up-to-date information about U.N. work in areas like peace and security, economic and social development, and human rights; and browse press releases and daily highlights, often before printed versions are released. You can also get free publications (in several languages) from the U.N. and many of its agencies and programs.

YANKEE STADIUM

It's the House that Ruth Built—Babe Ruth, that is—as well as the Home of the Champions. (The Yankees hold 26 world titles.) Since April 18, 1923, when the team played its first game here—against the Boston Red Sox—the Yankees have captivated this town and played many exciting baseball games at the stadium.

Take them out to the ball game, but come a little early. The park opens up 1½–2 hours before each game, and kids can often score an autograph from a player before the end of batting practice, if they move close to the field. Before the game is also a great time to tour Monument Park, which contains plaques and memorials to the all-time greats: Mickey Mantle, Joe DiMaggio, Lou Gehrig, and the Babe.

What fan wouldn't want to walk the field where Jeter and Giambi play ball? And who wouldn't want to enter the inner sanctum of the clubhouse to learn the tradition of the team's fabled uniform? Want to warm the seat where Williams and Rodriguez wait for their

EATS FOR KIDS Buy them some peanuts and Cracker Jacks. Kids won't care if they never get back! Typical ballpark fare is sold for sky-high prices, so bring clear bags (so security can view) of snacks from home and sit back and enjoy the vendors singing their sales pitch.

HEY, KIDS! Want to celebrate your birthday at Yankee Stadium? For $35 per person, you can have a 1¾-hour Birthday Bash, including a nifty souvenir, a film on Yankee history in the Hall of Fame Suite, soda, pizza, and cake. Ever wonder about the big-screen messages on the fan marquee, that flashy screen in right center? Ten different messages, including birthday wishes and marriage proposals, can appear on the screen for $100, or for a mere $10 you can put Happy Birthday, Happy Anniversary, Congratulations, or just Hi on the centerfield scoreboard. Proceeds from these fun shout-outs go to the New York Yankees Foundation, which supports area youth programs.

44 E. 161st St., Bronx

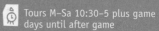 Games $8–$95; tours $12–$25 ages 15 and up, $6–$15 children 14 and under

Tours M–Sa 10:30–5 plus game days until after game

718/293–4300, 718/298–6000 tours; www.newyorkyankees.com

 5 and up

turn at bat? Even when there's no game at Yankee Stadium, the allure of a tour will delight any baseball aficionado, young or old. Choose from three tours. The Classic Tour is a one-hour Yankees history lesson with a visit to the dugout, the press box, and Monument Park. The Champions Tour, 20 minutes longer, includes all of that plus a visit to the clubhouse and a short film in the Adidas Suite. The Champions Plus Tour, 1 hour and 35 minutes, includes all of the above plus a stop in the Great Moments room, a luxury suite in the Yankee clubhouse. When there's no game, you can park free at parking lot 14, the players' lot, across from the press gate.

KEEP IN MIND Children under 30 inches tall who can walk under a turnstile or can be carried in can attend games free, but they must sit in your lap. There are baby-changing facilities in women's and some men's bathrooms on the Field, Main, Loge, and Tier levels. Guest Services provides wristbands to help children identify their seat locations. If lost, children are taken to the Yankee lobby on the Field Level near the Press Gate. Alcohol-free family sections are located in Tier reserved sections 13 and 14. Steer clear of the "bleacher creatures" in the cheap seats. These fans are not known for good clean fun.

CLASSIC GAMES

"I SEE SOMETHING YOU DON'T SEE, AND IT IS BLUE." Stuck for a way to get your youngsters to settle down in a museum? Sit them down on a bench in the middle of a room and play this vintage favorite. The leader gives just one clue—the color—and everybody guesses away.

"I'M GOING TO THE GROCERY ..." The first player begins, "I'm going to the grocery and I'm going to buy . . ." and finishes the sentence with the name of an object that begins with the letter "A" and is found in grocery stores. The second player repeats what the first player has said, and adds the name of another item that starts with "B." The third player repeats everything that has been said so far and adds something that begins with "C" and so on through the alphabet. Anyone who skips or misremembers an item is out (or decide up front that you'll give hints to all who need 'em). You can modify the theme depending on where you're going that day, as "I'm going to X and I'm going to see . . ."

FAMILY ARK Noah had his ark—here's your chance to build your own. It's easy. Just start naming animals and work your way through the alphabet, from antelope to zebra.

PLAY WHILE YOU WAIT

NOT THE GOOFY GAME Have one child name a category. (Some ideas: first names, last names, animals, countries, friends, feelings, foods, hot or cold things, clothing.) Then take turns naming things that fall into that category. You're out if you name something that doesn't belong in the category—or if you can't think of another item to name. When only one person remains, start again. Choose categories depending on where you're going or where you've been—historic topics if you've seen a historic sight, animal topics before or after the zoo, upside-down things if you've been to the circus, and so on. Make the game harder by choosing category items in A-B-C order.

DRUTHERS How do your kids really feel about things? Just ask. "Would you rather eat worms or hamburgers? Hamburgers or candy?" Choose serious and silly topics—and have fun!

BUILD A STORY "Once upon a time there lived . . ." Finish the sentence and ask the rest of your family, one at a time, to add another sentence or two. Bring a tape recorder along to record the narrative—and you can enjoy your creation again and again.

GOOD TIMES GALORE

WIGGLE & GIGGLE Give your kids a chance to stick out their tongues at you. Start by making a face, then have the next person imitate you and add a gesture of his own—snapping fingers, winking, clapping, sneezing, or the like. The next person mimics the first two and adds a third gesture, and so on.

JUNIOR OPERA During a designated period of time, have your kids sing everything they want to say.

THE QUIET GAME Need a good giggle—or a moment of calm to figure out your route? The driver sets a time limit and everybody must be silent. The last person to make a sound wins.

HIGH FIVES

BEST IN TOWN
Bronx Zoo
New York Botanical Garden
Central Park
New York Hall of Science
Ellis Island

BEST OUTDOORS
Rye Playland

BEST CULTURAL ACTIVITY
Broadway on a Budget

BEST MUSEUM
American Museum of Natural History

WACKIEST
Sony Wonder Technology Lab

NEW & NOTEWORTHY
The completely renovated Museum of Modern Art

SOMETHING FOR EVERYONE

ART ATTACK
American Folk Art Museum 68
Brooklyn Museum 59
Children's Museum of the Arts 52
Forbes Magazine Galleries 44
Jewish Museum 40
Metropolitan Museum of Art 34
Museum of Modern Art 33
National Museum of the American Indian 30

COOL 'HOODS
Broadway on a Budget 64
Lower East Side Tenement Museum 37
South Street Seaport Museum 7

FARMS AND ANIMALS
Bronx Zoo 63
Central Park Zoo 55
Claremont Riding Academy 51
Prospect Park Zoo 16
Queens County Farm Museum 14
Queens Zoo 13
Staten Island Zoo 5

FREEBIES
Clay Pit Ponds State Park Preserve 50
Forbes Magazine Galleries 44
National Museum of the American Indian 30
Queens County Farm Museum 14
Schomburg Center 9
Sony Wonder Technology Lab 8
Castle Clinton National Monument 57

GAMES AND AMUSEMENTS
Chelsea Piers 54
Coney Island 48
Rye Playland 10

GOOD SPORTS
Asphalt Green 65
Chelsea Piers 54
Claremont Riding Academy 51
Madison Square Garden 35
New York Liberty Basketball 20

ALL AROUND TOWN

MANY THANKS

I n the '70s, my boyfriend—now husband—and I would joke that we were off on another "family adventure" as we explored parks, museums, and other attractions. No family, of course. Today, more than a quarter of a century later, we still take those family adventures, but now with three children in tow. As a parent, a teacher, and writer, I look for those "teachable moments" to share with my children. I must confess that with a 5-year-old, a 12-year-old, and a 14-year-old, it is often challenging to find something of interest for everyone, parents included. This book was written with that in mind.

Many thanks to the public relations professionals at each of our sights who were so helpful in answering questions and checking facts. This book is lovingly dedicated to Rachel ("Are we there yet?"); Jennifer ("Can we listen to the car radio instead of those children's tapes?"); and Michael ("When are we leaving?").

— Mindy Bailin